The ESL Reader's Companion to

Of Mice and Men

by John Steinbeck

Linda Butler

The McGraw-Hill Companies, Inc.

New York St. Louis San Francisco Auckland Bogotá
Caracas Lisbon London Madrid Mexico Milan Montreal
New Delhi San Juan Singapore Sydney Tokyo Toronto

This book is dedicated with love to Miles and Claire and Jim.

A Division of The McGraw·Hill Companies

The ESL Reader's Companion to "Of Mice and Men"

Copyright © 1996 by The McGraw-Hill Companies, Inc. All rights reserved. Printed in the United States of America. Except as permitted under the United States Copyright Act of 1976, no part of this publication may be reproduced or distributed in any form or by any means, or stored in a database or retrieval system, without the prior written permission of the publisher.

3 4 5 6 7 8 9 0   FGR FGR 9 0 9 8 7

ISBN 0-07-009427-6

Sponsoring editor: Tim Stookesberry
Production supervisor: Natalie Durbin
Project management: Fritz/Brett Associates
Copy editor: Susan Defosset
Cover design: Elizabeth Williamson
Interior design: Rogondino & Associates
Compositor: Pat Rogondino
Illustrator: Tara Winkler
Printer and binder: Quebecor Printing Fairfield, Inc.

Library of Congress Catalog Card Number 96-75135

The passages from the novel used in this book are from OF MICE AND MEN by John Steinbeck. Copyright John Steinbeck, 1937. Copyright renewed John Steinbeck, 1965. Used by permission of Penguin Books USA Inc.

The excerpts on pages 36–38 and 62–65 are from OF MICE AND MEN: A PLAY IN THREE ACTS by John Steinbeck, 1937. Reprinted by permission of Viking Press, a division of Penguin Books USA Inc.

All dictionary entries that appear in this book are reprinted by permission from THE NEWBURY HOUSE DICTIONARY OF AMERICAN ENGLISH. Copyright© 1996 by Heinle & Heinle Publishers, an International Thomson Publishing Company.

CONTENTS

PREFACE

The ESL Reader's Companion to Of Mice and Men is a workbook and guide that will help ESL/EFL students to understand and enjoy the novel, and will enhance their language learning as they do so.

The *Companion* is appropriate for students in university, secondary school, or adult ESOL programs. It offers the support needed especially by students who:

- Have not yet read extensively in English, or

- Are making the transition from materials written expressly for learners of English, or

- Do not usually read for pleasure in their first language.

Full-length novels present an excellent resource for learners of English. These works expose students to a great quantity of authentic written English where the language is true to a particular setting and particular relationships. Literature can provide the basis for lively discussion, thoughtful writing, vocabulary building, and cultural understanding—along with all the pleasures of a good story!

Of Mice and Men by John Steinbeck, winner of the 1962 Nobel Prize, concerns two itinerant laborers in California during the Great Depression. They share an unusual friendship and the dream of one day having some land and a house of their own. The story takes place on a ranch in the Salinas Valley where for the first time their dream seems to be within reach.

This *Companion* can be used with any edition of the novel, but the page numbers given in it refer to the Penguin Books edition (ISBN 0–1401–7739–6) published by Penguin Books USA Inc., 375 Hudson Street, New York, NY 10014.

ORGANIZATION OF THE *COMPANION*

The *Companion* begins with information about the language used in the novel, before-the-novel discussion questions (Starting Out), and a map of the area where the story takes place. The *Companion* chapters correspond to the chapters in the novel, and are divided into the following sections:

Before You Read

This section contains cultural and historical information and explanations of words or expressions that are archaic, colloquial, or non-standard, so students need not waste time hunting for them in their dictionaries. Like any novel with realistic dialogue, *Of Mice and Men* includes language that is inappropriate for students' own use.

On Your Own

This section contains basic comprehension questions about characters and events as well as questions that ask for readers' personal opinions. It ends with an invitation to students to write any questions they would like to ask the instructor about the novel.

Scene from the Novel

In this section are excerpts from Acts I and II of *Of Mice and Men: A Play in Three Acts* by John Steinbeck, which students can read aloud. There are also directions in Chapter 4 for creating a script for a scene.

Discussion

This section provides more challenging questions about the novel. Some questions send readers delving into the text to analyze it, to synthesize information, and to find support for their opinions. Other questions address issues raised by the novel and ask readers to share their thoughts.

Suggestions for Writing

Each of the three elements in this section will further students' understanding of the reading and help develop their English writing skills.

Personal Response   Students can keep a journal in which they comment on whatever they choose about the story.

Summarizing   Students can develop their skills at writing summaries through a variety of exercises.

Points of Departure   The topics given here are based on themes from the novel. Some focus on the novel itself, others on personal experiences.

Words to Know

From each part of the novel, ten to sixteen words or phrases have been chosen that are important for students to know. These words may be:

- Essential to understanding a key element in the novel,
- Familiar to students as having one meaning but used differently in the novel, and/or
- Valuable additions to students' general knowledge of English.

The words are presented in the context of sentences about the novel. The exercises provide the repeated exposures to words that help learners understand and remember them, plus a mini-review of the story. Answers appear in the Answer Key on page 137.

The *Companion* also includes the following sections:

About Quoting

The conventions of quoting are introduced here, followed by practice exercises based on the novel. The instructions to the student show the Modern Language Association format used in U.S. colleges and universities for papers in English and the humanities.

Test Yourself

Each of these sections provides a review of Words to Know studied earlier in the *Companion*. Answers appear in the Answer Key.

Concluding Sections

The *Companion* concludes with an Answer Key, Teaching Suggestions, and a complete list of the Words to Know.

ACKNOWLEDGMENTS

I would like to thank many people who helped in the creation of this book:

Juli Dulmage, Glenn Dulmage, Laura Dehler-Seter, and their ESL students at the Northfield Mount Hermon School (MA); Eileen Kelley and her ESL students at Holyoke Community College (MA); the faculty and staff of the International Language Institute of Massachusetts in Northampton; Irene Papoulis, Jean Bernard Johnston, and Elizabeth Coombs for their feedback and encouragement; Frances P. de Cordova, State Literacy Missions Consultant, BGCO (OK); Kara Garrett, Big Bend Community College (WA); and Margaret W. Puck, Palomar College (CA), for their reviews of preliminary versions of these materials; Margaret Metz and the entire sales and marketing staff of McGraw-Hill for their promotional efforts; the McGraw-Hill editorial team of Tim Stookesberry, Gina Martinez, Pam Tiberia, Bill Preston, and Thalia Dorwick for their support and guidance; and Jane Sloan for her invaluable assistance. I would also like to thank my colleagues in TESOL for generously sharing their expertise at conferences through the years.

TO THE STUDENT

First of all, congratulations! You have reached a point in your language learning where you are ready to read a novel written for native speakers of English. It is quite an accomplishment to have come so far. Now, to help you further along on your way, here is a "Companion."

The aim of this book is to increase your understanding of the novel *Of Mice and Men* and your pleasure in reading it. In addition, it will help you expand your vocabulary.

So now, let's begin!

ABOUT THE LANGUAGE OF THE NOVEL

When you read *Of Mice and Men,* you will notice that John Steinbeck has written much of the novel in the form of dialogue, or conversation, between the characters. To give these characters real voices—to make them come alive on the page for the reader—Steinbeck has written what they say in the way they would say it. That is, he has used the language typical of people in that place and at that time, and he has spelled some words in the way they are pronounced.

For example, in the novel (and often in informal American speech today), words that end in "-ing" are pronounced "-in" instead: "going" becomes **goin'** and "talking" becomes **talkin'**. You will soon become accustomed to this pattern.

Sometimes words are pronounced without their final sound. Steinbeck uses an apostrophe (') to signal that the last letter is missing, as in **jus'** (just), **spen'** (spend), **an'** (and), and **nex'** (next). Most of these will be easy for you to guess.

Some other changes in spelling that Steinbeck uses also reflect pronunciation:

gonna (going to)	**kinda** (kind of)
gotta (got to)	**musta** (must have)
oughta (ought to)	**ya** (you)

The sound of the letter "h" in the words "he," "him," "her," and "his" is often missing when Americans say these words. So Steinbeck writes:

"I had **'im** ever since he was a pup."

The speakers in the novel also omit words, especially subject pronouns (such as "I," "you," and "he") and auxiliary verbs (such as "am," "is," "are," and "have"). Here are some examples:

"[It] Looks kinda scummy."

"[He] Didn't wanta stop at the ranch gate."

"[Do you] Think I'd let you carry your own work card?"

"[I'll] Tell you what he used to do . . ."

You will also see words that are commonly used in the United States but are not acceptable in the standard English used in schools or universities. For example, Steinbeck often uses the word **ain't**, which can mean "am not," "is not," "are not," "have not," or "has not":

"I **ain't** sure." (I'm not sure.)

"I **ain't** got nothing." (I haven't got anything.)

"**Ain't** a thing in my pocket." (There isn't a thing . . .)

And finally, you will find that the characters in this novel swear. That is, they use words like "hell," "God damn," and "bastard." Sometimes these words are used to express anger but not always. They are just part of the everyday vocabulary of these characters. (None of these swear words are included in the vocabulary lists and exercises in this *Companion*.)

As a learner of English, you may wonder why a novel with so much nonstandard English has been recommended to you. But *Of Mice and Men* is very much worth reading by ESL students: John Steinbeck is a great American writer, and in this short novel he has written a powerful story. Reading *Of Mice and Men*, learning new vocabulary, and writing and talking about the novel will surely contribute to your mastery of English.

STARTING OUT

1. On page 2, you will see a map of the area of California where this story takes place. The following names of places appear in the story. Can you locate them on the map?

    Weed
    Soledad
    the Salinas River
    the Gabilan Mountains

2. Much of the story takes place on a ranch.

    - Have you ever been on a ranch?

    - Have you seen ranches in American movies that are set in the West?

    - What do you see in your "mind's eye" when you imagine a ranch? Make a list of what you see.

3. Think about the people living on ranches.

    - What kinds of work do they do?

    - What do they look like?

    - What are they like?

    - Where do your ideas and information about them come from?

4. Answer this question in writing: How do you feel about reading a novel in English?
    Share what you have written and talk about these feelings with a partner or a group of classmates.

Where the Story Takes Place

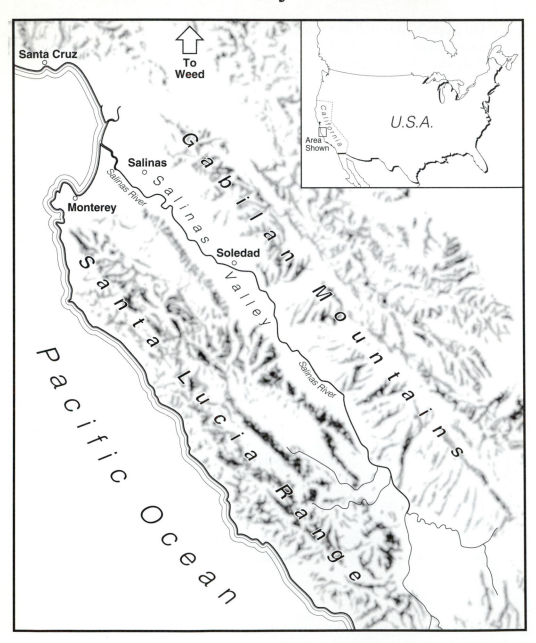

❧ Chapter One: Part One ❧

(pages 1–7)

BEFORE YOU READ

Take a look at the following words and expressions. They may be new to you, and they may not be in your dictionary. Some of them will be familiar to you, but in these instances carry different meanings from what you would expect; others are not commonly used in standard American English today.

You *do not* need to memorize these words and expressions, but you *do* need to understand them as they are used in the story.

PAGE

1   **the night tracks of 'coons** = prints left in the sand by the paws of raccoons that come down to the river at night

2   **tramps** = poor men with no homes or regular jobs who travel around from one place to another

jungle-up = set up camp for the night

3   **bindle** = rolled up blanket, extra clothes

ain't = am not, is not ("Ain't" is nonstandard English. See *Companion* page viii.)

5   **work cards** = cards that identify workers as being sent by an employment agency to a place of work (This novel was written during the Great Depression, a time of severe unemployment in the U.S., lasting from about 1929 to about 1939.)

6   **we're set** = we're OK, we're in a secure position

Ya got that? = Do you understand?

That's swell. = That's wonderful.

ON YOUR OWN

Reading

Read pages 1– 7 *without stopping.*

Don't worry about understanding every word—just try to get the main idea of what is happening.

When you finish, take out your dictionary and use it when necessary as you reread these pages. At this time, you can begin writing your reactions to the story in a reading journal. (See Suggestions for Writing, Personal Response, page 8.)

 Marking Your Book

Try rereading these pages with pen or pencil in hand. Then you can mark your book—underline words or sentences, or make notes in the margins.

A Closer Look

Write your answers to the following questions in the spaces provided.

1. Describe the two men camping by the river. What do they look like?

   George

   Lennie

2. George and Lennie are on their way to new jobs. What kind of work will they be doing?

3. What does Lennie try to hide from George? Why?

4. What instructions does George give Lennie about meeting the boss at the ranch?

5. What have you learned so far about a place called Weed?

Did anything in this chapter confuse you? Would you like to know more about something?

Write any questions you have about this chapter on a separate piece of paper and give it to your teacher. Your teacher might answer it or might tell you, "Wait—that's coming in the story." Or maybe the answer to your question is something that you must decide for yourself.

◄○► ⧉ ◄○►

The title "Of Mice and Men" does not refer to the mice Lennie likes to pet. It comes from a poem by Robert Burns, "To a Mouse On Turning Her Up in Her Nest with a Plow, November, 1785." The poem speaks of "the best laid schemes o' mice and men." Later on in this *Companion,* you'll read more about it.

DISCUSSION

Through talking with other readers, your ideas about the novel may change. Sometimes your ideas will come into focus more clearly when you speak about them. And sometimes others will voice the same thoughts you had and make you feel more sure of your ideas.

But in discussion, you might also hear something that makes you see the novel differently. Then you can reread those pages and rethink your ideas.

In some cases, all readers should get the same information from the novel. But at other times, there can be more than one good interpretation. Novels are like that: just as readers each come to a story with varied life experiences and beliefs, readers can come away from a story with different understandings of it.

So you will find different kinds of questions in each Discussion section. Some questions will have one good answer that your group must discover and agree on, while other questions can have more than one good answer.

1. What things do you notice that make you think there is something strange about Lennie?

2. How would you describe the way George treats Lennie?

3. Why do you think George and Lennie are together?

4. What do you think might have happened in Weed? List some possibilities.

5. With a partner, choose a phrase, a sentence, or a group of sentences that made an impression on both of you. One of you should read it aloud; then discuss it. In a group, have one partner tell the page number and place on the page of your selection, and then read it aloud. The other partner explains why the two of you chose it.

SUGGESTIONS FOR WRITING

Personal Response

Begin a reading journal for *Of Mice and Men.* Keep one notebook or folder just for this purpose.

You can make an entry in your journal after you finish your nonstop reading of a chapter, or while you are rereading it. You can add to an entry after discussion in class.

To make an entry, draw a line down a page in your notebook. To the left of that line, write down anything from the chapter that makes an impression on you. You can copy words or sentences from the novel or use your own words. Write down whatever *you* notice and want to comment on.

To the right of the line, write your reaction to what you wrote on the left. Did it confuse you? Surprise you? Did it make you smile? Make you angry? Perhaps it reminded you of something from your own life or something else you'd read.

Here is what one student, Tseng Chien Tuan, wrote as his journal entry for pages 1–7 of the novel:

What I noticed	What I thought
page 4 "O.K. – O.K. I'll tell ya again."	Lennie is so stupid! He makes George lose his patience.
page 5 "Ain't a thing in my pocket."	Lennie isn't so stupid. At least, he knows if George notices the mouse, he'll throw it out. Lennie's weird, keeping a dead mouse.
page 7 "God, you're a lot of trouble."	George and Lennie's relationship is very strange. Lennie causes trouble and George is still traveling with him. Maybe they are brothers or cousins.
the descriptions	The author's descriptions of places and people are very good. I can see the picture the author tries to describe very easily. The only thing I don't like about this book is that people swear too much.

Each of your journal entries may look different, as you notice and respond—with just a word or with a whole paragraph—to different aspects of the story and your experience reading it.

WORDS TO KNOW

Some of the words listed here are important to add to your general knowledge of English. Some will be important to know as you continue to read the novel.

The part of speech for each word is given after the word. What do these abbreviations stand for?

n. = _____ *v.* = _____ *adj.* = _____ *adv.* = _____

Learning New Words

If a word is new to you,

1. Look at the sentence to see how it is used. You can also look back at its use in the novel.
2. Guess at the meaning.
3. Check your dictionary—were you right?
4. Take notes about the word.

PAGE

1 **brush** *(n.)* Rabbits often come out of the **brush** in the evening, and they sit on the sandy river bank.

Your notes here →

a path *(n.)* A **path** through the trees and brush leads down to the Salinas River.

2 **emerge** *(v.)* Two men came down the path and **emerged** into the clearing by the river.

denim *(n.)* Both men wore **denim** trousers and coats.

a paw *(n.)* The big man dragged his feet a bit as he walked, like a bear dragging its **paws**.

4   **imitate** *(v.)* Lennie watched George closely and **imitated** him.

morosely *(adv.)* George sat down near the water's edge, stared **morosely** at the river, and then spoke angrily.

scowl *(v.)* George **scowled**, showing his annoyance with Lennie.

5   **grin** *(v.)* Lennie **grinned** in relief to know that he had not lost his work card—George had it.

6   **pet** *(v.)* Lennie liked to **pet** the dead mouse with his thumb while he and George walked along.

Exercise 1   Write each word next to its definition.

brush   a path   a paw

1. _____ a track or trail for walking along

2. _____ the foot of an animal with claws or nails

3. _____ bushes, small trees, and other plants

Exercise 2   Use one of the following words to complete each sentence about the story. Change word forms as necessary.

> **denim   emerge   grin   imitate   morosely   scowl**

1. George and Lennie came down a path from the highway to the river. Coming out of the trees and brush, they _____ into a clearing by the water.
   (past)

2. The two men wore pants and jackets made of _____.

3. Lennie watched George so that he could _____ him. He liked to do the same things George did.

4. George was angry at the bus driver, so he was in a bad mood. He sat and stared _____ at the river.

5. When Lennie made George angry and impatient, George _____ at him.
   (past)

6. When Lennie was happy, he _____.
   (past)

Exercise 3   Use the same words to complete the following sentences. These sentences do *not* relate to the story, so you will see each word used in another context.

> **denim   emerge   grin   imitate   morosely   scowl**

1. Have you seen that comedian on TV who can _____ the President? He sounds just like him!

2. When someone is smiling with great delight, we might say that this person is _____ "from ear to ear."
   (–ing)

3. My brother was depressed about failing his exam. I tried to cheer him up, but he just sat _____ at his desk with his head in his hands and wouldn't speak to me.

4. My roommate hates waking up. I smile and say, "Good morning!", but she just _____ and says nothing.
   (–s)

5. Blue jeans are made of _____.

6. The police surrounded the building and waited for the suspects to
_____.

> **pet**
>
> a. *(n.)* a tame animal kept in the home and treated with
>   kindness and affection
> b. *(n.)* a favorite person
> c. *(v.)* to stroke lightly and fondly with the hand
>
>   From *The Newbury House Dictionary of American English*

Exercise 4 Look at the box above. Which meaning does "pet" have in
each of the following sentences? Write the letter of the definition next to
each sentence.

____*a*____ **1.** My neighbors have an unusual **pet**: a tarantula!

_____ **2.** I like to **pet** my cat.

_____ **3.** That girl's classmates dislike her; they think she's "the
teacher's **pet**."

Exercise 5 Are the underlined words in these sentences nouns or verbs?

noun **1.** I saw a <u>scowl</u> on his face.

_____ **2.** She smiled at him but he just <u>scowled</u>.

_____ **3.** Would you like to <u>pet</u> a rabbit?

_____ **4.** Dogs and cats are the most common <u>pets</u> in the U.S.

_____ **5.** A broad <u>grin</u> spread across his face.

_____ **6.** Why is everybody <u>grinning</u> at me?

❧ Chapter One: Part Two ❧

(pages 7–16)

BEFORE YOU READ

Take a look at the following words and expressions. They may be new to you and may not be in your dictionary. Some of them will be familiar to you but in these instances carry different meanings from what you would expect; others are not commonly used in standard American English today.

You *do not* need to memorize these expressions, but you *do* need to understand them as they are used in the story.

PAGE

7　**They run us outa Weed** = They forced us to leave Weed. They chased us out of town.

8　**thrashin' machine** = a thresher, a machine that separates the grains or seeds of a plant (the parts of the plant which are used as food) from the stalks (which are not eaten)

　bustin' a gut = doing very hard physical work

　You ain't puttin' nothing over. = You aren't fooling me.

11　**a cat house** = a house of prostitution

　An' whatta I got = And what have I got?

　in hot water = in trouble

12　**go nuts** = become crazy

13　**You get a kick outta that** = You get pleasure out of that

　work up a stake = earn and save money

　blow their stake = waste their savings

14　**jack** = money

　live off the fatta the lan' = "live off the fat of the land," live in ease and comfort with what the land produces

ON YOUR OWN

Reading

Read the rest of the chapter *without stopping*.

Don't worry about understanding every word—just try to get the main idea of what is happening.

When you finish, take out your dictionary and use it when necessary as you reread these pages. At this time, you can begin an entry in your reading journal. (See Suggestions for Writing, Personal Response, page 19.)

 Marking Your Book

You can mark words or sentences by underlining, circling, or highlighting them. You can also draw stars or arrows in the margin. But *don't* write between the lines. It can distract your eye when you reread. Instead, make your notes in the margins.

A Closer Look

Write your answers to the following questions in the spaces provided.

1. What does Lennie remember about his Aunt Clara?

2. According to George, how are he and Lennie different from most men who work on ranches?

3. What is George and Lennie's plan for the future?

4. Do you believe George and Lennie will succeed? Why or why not?

5. If Lennie gets into trouble on the ranch to which they are going, where is he supposed to go?

6. Have you heard the expression "The American Dream"? Ask several people who are familiar with American culture what this expression means. Write down their answers and bring them to class.

   Write any questions *you* have about this chapter.

DISCUSSION

1. How would you describe Lennie? What does he do and say that gives you this impression of him?

2. What kind of trouble has Lennie gotten into in the past?

3. Do you agree or disagree with this statement:

   George and Lennie's lifestyle allows them a lot of freedom.

   Give reasons for your answer.

4. What is "The American Dream"? Compare the explanations of this expression that each of you has collected.

SUGGESTIONS FOR WRITING

Personal Response

Make an entry in your reading journal.

Here is the entry that one student, Jessie Chang, made in her journal after reading Chapter 1 of the novel:

What I noticed	What I thought
p. 7 "The day was going fast now."	When you are enjoying the time, you'll feel the time passes very fast. However, if you are doing something you don't like to do, you'll find out that it seems like there is no limit there.
p. 8 "Poor bastard, he said softly."	George said "bastard" softly which means he didn't really mean Lennie is a bastard even though he said that. That's really confusing.
p. 11 "You can't keep a job and you lose me ever' job I get."	I think they have been together for a long time and George takes care of Lennie, not reluctantly.
p. 12 Lennie says he'll go away and leave George alone.	Lennie finally understands that he's really annoying. But I think he's smart that he knows George will never let him go away. I have to say that Lennie is cute, in some way. His mind is like a five-year-old child's (the mouse, forgetting everything, the ketchup). Who knows what will happen tomorrow? But my feelings tell me that they will meet a lot of troubles in the future (just like every single novel and movie).

Summarizing

Read the following summary of this chapter.

Summary A   In the first chapter of *Of Mice and Men,* we meet two men who are camping for the night by the Salinas River. One man, George, is small and quick, while the other man, Lennie, is very big and seems stupid. He forgets everything, and George has to remind him that they are on their way to work on a ranch. He yells at Lennie for always getting into trouble, and he tells him what to do at this next job. Before they go to sleep, Lennie gets George to talk about their plan to have a little ranch of their own someday, a place where Lennie will get to tend rabbits.

Compare the following two summaries with summary A. As you read them, think about what information belongs in a summary and what information does not.

Summary B   In this chapter, we meet two men who are on their way to new jobs. I think they are friends, but maybe they are relatives. They are spending the night camping by a river. The small one is always telling the big one what to do. In my opinion, he treats him like a slave. However, the big one is not very smart, he can't remember anything, and sometimes he does stupid things. The small one gets mad and yells at him, but then he calms down. The two men eat, talk, and then go to sleep.

Summary C   Two men, George and Lennie, walk down a path to a river where they set up camp. George tells Lennie to get wood for the fire. Lennie can't remember where they are going, and he keeps a dead mouse in his pocket, and he keeps saying he likes ketchup on his beans. He asks George why they are eating here and not at the ranch. George yells at Lennie, "You keep me in hot water all the time," but then he is sorry. He describes how they are going to have a little house and a cow, pigs, rabbits, and chickens.

Look for the following problems in summaries B and C. Next to each problem, write B, C, or B and C.

1. _____ The summary is too general; it needs more specific information.

2. _____ The summary has unnecessary details.

3. _____ The writer hasn't explained the main ideas of the chapter; instead, the summary is only a list of details.

4. _____ The writer has included a personal opinion in the summary.

5. _____ The writer hasn't identified what is being summarized.

Points of Departure

In this section, you will find ideas to write about. Your teacher may ask you to write about one in your journal, or as a freewriting exercise, or in the form of an essay.

1. Can you think of a pair of friends you have known who are very different from each other, or who have an unusual friendship? Write a description of these two friends. How are they different? What makes them friends?

2. Do you ever imagine the perfect place to live? Where would it be, and what would it be like? Who would live there with you? How would you spend your time?

   Write in detail about your idea of the perfect place to live. You can describe a place that can exist only in your imagination, or you can write about a home that may one day be a dream come true.

WORDS TO KNOW

Study these words if they are new to you.

✏️ **Learning New Words**

1. Look at the sentence to see how the word is used.
2. Guess at the meaning.
3. Look it up.
4. Take notes.

PAGE

7 **remind** *(v.)* George didn't want to **remind** Lennie about what had happened in Weed.

disgustedly *(adv.)* George spoke **disgustedly** of how they had run away.

9 **reluctantly** *(adv.)* **Reluctantly**, Lennie put his hand into his pocket to get the mouse.

stroke *(v.)* Lennie had enjoyed **stroking** the mouse.

11 **sneak** *(v.)* George described how they had to **sneak** out of Weed under cover of darkness.

ashamedly *(adv.)* Knowing he had hurt Lennie's feelings, George looked **ashamedly** at the campfire.

12   **a cave** *(n.)* Lennie offered to go into the hills and live in a **cave** so that he wouldn't bother George anymore.

mean *(adj.)* George knew that he had been **mean** to Lennie.

14   **look after** *(v.)* Lennie talked about how he and George **looked after** each other.

by heart *(adv. phrase)* Lennie knew the story **by heart**, but he still wanted to hear George tell it.

tend *(v.)* Lennie looks forward to **tending** the rabbits when he and George get a place of their own.

Exercise 1   Use one of the following words or phrases to complete each sentence about the story. You will need to change the form of one word.

by heart   cave   look after   remind   sneak   tend

1.   George didn't want to _____ Lennie of the trouble he had caused in Weed because he was afraid that if Lennie remembered, he might do it again.

2.   George and Lennie _____ out of Weed after dark.

3.   Lennie offered to go away and leave George alone. He said he would go off into the mountains and live in a _____.

4.   George and Lennie believe they aren't like other men who work on ranches because they take care of each other. *Lennie* says happily, *"I got you to _____ me . . ."* (14).

5.   Lennie likes to hear George talk about the land they are going to have, even though he knows the story _____.

6.   Lennie's dream is to _____ rabbits on their own little ranch.

Exercise 2   Use the same words to complete the following sentences, which are *not* related to the story. You will need to change the forms of two words.

by heart   cave   look after   remind   sneak   tend

1.   My neighbor is a bartender in a restaurant downtown. He _____ the bar there, mixing and serving drinks.

2.   Parents sometimes ask older brothers and sisters to _____ younger ones.

3.   If you go into a _____, you need to take a flashlight or torch so that you can see.

4.   Actors practice their lines for a play until they have them _____.

5.   I write notes to _____ myself of things I need to remember to do.

6.   The two boys didn't have tickets for the baseball game, so they tried to _____ into the ballpark.

Exercise 3   Choose the adjective or adverb form of each word.

disgusted   disgustedly

1.   George spoke in a _____ voice of how they left Weed.

2.   He shook his head _____ remembering how they had run.

reluctant   reluctantly

3.   Lennie reached into his pocket slowly and _____.

4.   He was _____ to give up his mouse.

ashamed   ashamedly

5.   George felt _____ of himself for yelling at Lennie.

6.   When he saw how much he had hurt Lennie's feelings, he looked down _____.

---

stroke

a. *(v.)* to pass the hand lightly over [something]

b. *(n.)* a motion of a body part from one position to another, done in a sport to move or hit [something]

c. *(n.)* a blocked or broken blood vessel in the brain that causes a lack of muscle control, difficulty speaking, and sometimes death

From *The Newbury House Dictionary of American English*

Exercise 4   Look at the box above. Which meaning does "stroke" have in each of the following sentences? Write the letter of the definition next to each sentence.

_____ 1. The swimmers raced through the water with hard, fast **strokes**.

_____ 2. After my grandmother's **stroke**, she couldn't speak.

_____ 3. Have you ever **stroked** a rabbit?

> **mean**
>
> a. *(v.)* to indicate, have significance
>
> b. *(v.)* to intend to, want to do [something]
>
> c. *(adj.)* wanting to hurt someone
>
> d. *(n.)* a number in the middle between two extremes of
> numbers
>
> From *The Newbury House Dictionary of American English*

Exercise 5   Look at the box above. Which meaning does "mean" have in each of the following sentences? Write the letter of the definition next to each sentence.

_____ **1.** My mother said, "Don't be **mean** to your little brother!"

_____ **2.** What does the word "sneak" **mean**?

_____ **3.** I **meant** to call you last night, but I forgot.

_____ **4.** The students' test scores varied widely, but the **mean** for the class was 72%.

ABOUT QUOTING

What Is Quoting?

When you answer questions about the story, sometimes you will want to write your answer by copying directly from the book. For example, here is a question about the first chapter of the novel:

How did Lennie imitate George?

You could write:

Lennie tried to sit like George. "He pushed himself back, drew up his knees, embraced them, looked over to George to see whether he had it just right". (4)

This would be a good answer. In this answer, you would be *quoting—copying the author's words.*

Or you could write:

Lennie watched the way George sat and the way he wore his hat, and then Lennie copied him.

This would be a good answer, too. You would be *using your own words.*

When Do We Quote?

We use quotations when using words of our own would create a problem. For example, using our own words might:

- Change the author's meaning, or
- Require writing many more words to say the same thing, or
- Mean losing a special effect or image the author has created.

It's good to write answers using your own words. That gives you valuable practice thinking about the reading and using your writing skills.

Sometimes, however, you have to quote. For example, you have to quote to answer this question about the first chapter:

> On page 2 of the novel, in what way does the author compare Lennie to an animal?

The best answer to this question would be something like this:

> Steinbeck writes that Lennie "walked heavily, dragging his feet a little, the way a bear drags his paws" (2).

How Do We Quote?

The following rules for quoting follow the format prescribed by the Modern Language Association (MLA):

1. Copy the author's words *exactly*.
2. Put quotation marks before the first word you copy and after the last word.
3. After the quotation marks, put the page number with parentheses around it.
4. Put a period after the final parenthesis.

For example:

Lennie "drank with long gulps, snorting into the water like a horse" (3).

When you quote words that are *already within quotation marks* in the book, then you must use a second set of quotation marks, called single quotation marks. For example:

Lennie admitted killing the mice that his Aunt Clara gave him:

" 'They was so little,' he said, apologetically" (9–10).

Here is another example:

Lennie offered to go away and leave George alone, but "George

said, 'I want you to stay with me, Lennie' " (13).

Exercise 1   Answer again question 1 from page 5 in the *Companion*: "Describe the two men camping by the river. What do they look like?" This time, use *your own words* to describe one man, and use a *quotation* to describe the other man.

George

Lennie

∽ Chapter Two: Part One ∾

(pages 17–28)

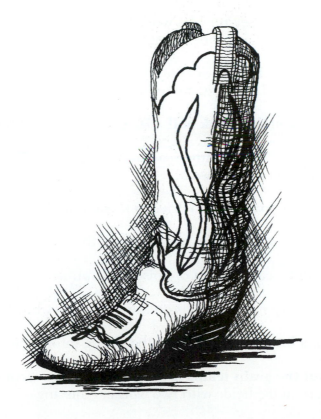

BEFORE YOU READ

Take a look at the following words and expressions.

17   **bunk house** = a rough, simple building with narrow beds

18   **sore as hell** = very angry

       pants rabbits, graybacks = insects that live on people

       the old swamper = the old man who does menial jobs

       blacksmith = a person who works with iron, shaping the hot metal into horseshoes, tools, etc.

19   **the stable buck** = the worker who takes care of horses and the equipment in the stable or barn

       he give the stable buck hell = He yelled angrily at him.

20   **a nigger** = an African-American or black person (This word is offensive. Do not use it.)

       a skinner = a person who drives a team of mules

       took after = attacked, started a fight with

       raised hell = caused a lot of noise and trouble

       spurs = sharp metal devices on the heels of cowboy boots

21   **gave us a bum steer** = gave us the wrong information

       send out the grain teams short two buckers = sent the men to work in the fields with two workers missing

22   **rassel** = wrestle, lift, move, manage

       a cultivator = a machine for loosening the ground to plant crops or remove weeds

a bale = a large bundle of hay, tightly packed and tied

Why ya think I'm sellin' him out? = Why do you think I'm cheating him?

23   **buck barley** = lift or carry heavy bags of grain

I seen wise guys before. = I know how to deal with men who think they are too smart for me.

leave your big flapper shut = keep your mouth closed

24   **nosey** = too curious about other people's personal business

26   **what the hell's he got on his shoulder?** = What is he so angry about? (This comes from the expression "to have a chip on one's shoulder," meaning to be full of resentment.)

Curley's pretty handy. = Curley's good at boxing.

the ring = the place where boxing matches are held

picking scraps = starting fights

S'pose Curley jumps a big guy an' licks him. = Imagine that Curley attacks a big man and beats him.

27   **canned** = fired from a job

cockier'n ever = more self-confident and conceited than ever

vaseline = petroleum jelly, an ointment or lubricant

28   **purty** = pretty

She got the eye = she looks at men in a way that shows sexual interest

tart = prostitute

ON YOUR OWN

Reading

Read pages 17–28 *without stopping.*

Don't worry about understanding every word—just try to get the main idea of what is happening.

When you finish, take out your dictionary and use it when necessary as you reread these pages.

Marking Your Dictionary

When you look up a word in your dictionary, make a dot with your pen in the margin next to it. If you find yourself looking up a word that already has three dots next to it, memorize it!

A Closer Look

1. It is the next morning. George and Lennie have arrived at the ranch and have been taken to the bunk house. Which word best describes the bunk house? Circle it.

    luxurious   comfortable   army-like   prison-like

    Why did you choose that word?

2. In this chapter, we meet several people who live on the ranch. What do you know so far about these two:

the swamper

Curley

3. We also hear about "the stable buck." What do you know about him?

4. Describe Candy's dog.

5. How do you think Candy feels about this dog?

6. What does George say will happen if Curley starts a fight with Lennie?

Write any questions *you* have about this chapter.

SCENE FROM THE NOVEL

The following scene is excerpted from *Of Mice and Men: A Play in Three Acts* by John Steinbeck (New York: The Viking Press, 1937), pages 41–44. You will need three people to read aloud the parts of the boss, George, and Lennie.

Before reading aloud, practice your role by reading your lines softly to yourself. If you are uncomfortable speaking the dialect of your character, you can make changes in your lines. For example, the boss asks, "Where you boys been workin'?" You could change this to "Where have you boys been working?" Be careful not to change the *meaning* of your character's words.

In this scene, all three men are standing, George facing the boss and Lennie a little off to the side. The boss opens a small notebook and prepares to write in it with his pencil.

BOSS: What's your name?

GEORGE: George Milton.

BOSS: George Milton. *Writing:* And what's yours?

GEORGE: His name's Lennie Small.

BOSS: Lennie Small. *Writing:* Le's see, this is the twentieth. Noon the twentieth. . . . *Makes positive mark. Closes the book and puts it in his pocket.* Where you boys been workin'?

GEORGE: Up around Weed.

BOSS: *to Lennie:* You too?

GEORGE: Yeah. Him too.

BOSS: *to Lennie:* Say, you're a big fellow, ain't you?

GEORGE: Yeah, he can work like hell, too.

BOSS: He ain't much of a talker, though, is he?

GEORGE: No, he ain't. But he's a hell of a good worker. Strong as a bull.

LENNIE: *smiling:* I'm strong as a bull. *George scowls at him and Lennie drops his head in shame at having forgotten.*

BOSS: *sharply:* You are, huh? What can you do?

GEORGE: He can do anything.

BOSS: *addressing Lennie:* What can you do? *Lennie, looking at George, gives a high nervous chuckle.*

GEORGE: *quickly:* Anything you tell him. He's a good skinner. He can wrestle grain bags, drive a cultivator. He can do anything. Just give him a try.

BOSS: *turning to George:* Then why don't you let *him* answer? *Lennie laughs.* What's he laughing about?

GEORGE: He laughs when he gets excited.

BOSS: Yeah?

GEORGE: *loudly:* But he's a goddamn good worker. I ain't saying he's bright, because he ain't. But he can put up a four hundred pound bale.

BOSS: *hooking his thumbs in his belt:* Say, what you sellin'?

GEORGE: Huh?

BOSS: I said what stake you got in this guy? You takin' his pay away from him?

GEORGE:	No. Of course I ain't!
BOSS:	[Well], I never seen one guy take so much trouble for another guy. I just like to know what your percentage is.
GEORGE:	He's my . . . cousin. I told his ole lady I'd take care of him. He got kicked in the head by a horse when he was a kid. He's all right. . . . Just ain't bright. But he can do anything you tell him.
BOSS:	*turning half away:* Well, God knows he don't need no brains to buck barley bags. *He turns back.* But don't you try to put nothing over, Milton. I got my eye on you.

DISCUSSION

1. What does the boss suspect George of doing? Why?

2. What is Curley's reaction to Lennie? Why does he act that way?

3. Are you curious about what will happen next in the story? Write down questions or predictions about what is going to happen. (If you have already read past page 28, please do not give away what you know about the story!)

SUGGESTIONS FOR WRITING

Personal Response

Make an entry in your reading journal. If you like to draw, think about adding sketches or cartoons to your journal. You might draw the bunk house, the ranch, or someone in the story. Write about what you have drawn in your own words, or label your drawings with quotes from the novel.

WORDS TO KNOW

An asterisk (*) marks irregular verbs.

PAGE

17   **scoff at** *(v.)* Steinbeck tells us that ranch men **scoff at** Western magazines but secretly believe the stories in them.

19   **skeptically** *(adv.)* George spoke **skeptically**, not trusting the old swamper's explanation.

20   **crooked** *(adj.)* The old man said the stable buck had a **crooked** back because he had been kicked by a horse.

21   **shuffle** *(v.)* When the boss came in, the old swamper **shuffled** to the door and went out.

22   **panic** *(n.)* Lennie, in a **panic** at the boss's question, looked to George for help.

bright *(adj.)* George admitted that Lennie wasn't **bright**.

a stake *(n.)* The boss asked George what **stake** he had in Lennie.

23   **get away with** *(v.)** The boss warned George not to try to **get away with** anything.

24   **struggle** *(v.)* The old dog had to **struggle** just to walk across the room.

reassure *(v.)* George calmed down, **reassured** that the old man hadn't heard George's conversation with Lennie.

25   **calculating** *(adj.)* Curley gave Lennie a **calculating** look.

squirm *(v.)* Lennie **squirmed** nervously because of the way Curley looked at him.

26   **stare** *(v.)* Curley **stared** at Lennie.

27   **show off** *(v.)** George suggested that Curley might be **showing off** for his new wife.

gossip *(n.)* The swamper enjoyed telling George the **gossip** about Curley and his wife.

derogatory *(adj.)* George made a **derogatory** remark about Curley when he heard what Curley had said about the vaseline.

Exercise 1 Write each word or phrase next to its definition.

scoff at   shuffle   squirm   show off

1. _____ try to get people's attention and admiration

2. _____ ridicule, make fun of, laugh at

3. _____ walk slowly without lifting the feet

4. _____ move or twist in discomfort or nervousness

Exercise 2 Use one of the following words or phrases to complete each sentence about the story. You will need to change the form of one word.

get away with   gossip   panic   reassure   stake   struggle

1. Lennie was filled with _____ when the boss questioned him. He didn't know what to say and he looked anxiously at George for help.

2. The boss wondered what _____ George had in Lennie. He was suspicious of George's interest in Lennie.

3. The boss warned George not to try to put anything over on him. His years of experience made him hard to fool, so he said George couldn't _____ anything.

4. The dog was so old and weak that he had to _____ to walk across the room.

5. George accused the old swamper of listening to him talk to Lennie. But Candy said he hadn't been listening—ranch hands know not to do that. This answer _____ George and he relaxed.

6. The old swamper was eager to pass on to George some _____ about Curley and his new wife.

Exercise 3 Use the same words and phrases to complete the following sentences, which are *not* related to the story. You will need to change the forms of two words.

get away with   gossip   panic   reassure   stake   struggle

1. I was nervous going to have my tooth pulled. But the dentist _____ me that it would not hurt as much as I feared.

2. When the young mother realized that her two-year-old son was no longer next to her in the store, she felt a sudden _____. Then she saw him looking at some toys.

3. Many Americans like to read _____ in magazines about the private lives of movie stars and other rich and famous people.

4. My neighbors have invested a lot of money in a new restaurant, so they have a great _____ in the success of the business.

5. The robbers stole $15,000 from the bank, but they didn't _____ their crime: they were arrested the next day.

6. I was so tired that I _____ to keep my eyes open and finish my homework.

Exercise 4 Do the underlined words in each pair of sentences have similar or different meanings? In the spaces, write "similar" or "different."

1. He <u>stared</u> at her.

   He <u>grinned</u> at her. _____

2. She's very <u>bright</u>.

   She's very <u>smart</u>. _____

3.   The line was <u>crooked</u>.

       The line was <u>straight</u>. _____

4.   It's a <u>derogatory</u> word.

       It's a <u>complimentary</u> word. _____

5.   He <u>reassured</u> me.

       He <u>calmed my fears.</u> _____

NOUNS	VERBS	ADJECTIVES	ADVERBS
a skeptic skepticism		skeptical	skeptically

Exercise 5   Look at the chart above for words related to "skeptically." Fill in each blank with the appropriate member of this word family.

1.   George was _____ when the old swamper claimed their beds were clean.

2.   He listened _____ to what the old man told him.

3.   "I ain't so sure," said George, greeting the swamper's explanation with _____.

4.   George was slow to believe what he was told. Do you think George is a _____ by nature?

NOUNS	VERBS	ADJECTIVES	ADVERBS
_____ _____	_____	calculating	

Exercise 6   Use your dictionary to complete the chart above. Then fill in each blank with the appropriate member of this word family. You will need to change the forms of two words.

1. Curley had a _____ look in his eye, thinking about what kind of fighter Lennie would be.

2. Curley probably _____ that he could beat Lennie in a fight.

3. A _____ can help a person solve math problems quickly.

4. All of the student's _____ on her physics exam were correct.

Exercise 7   What part of speech is the underlined word in each sentence?

_____ **1.** The old man got out of bed and <u>shuffled</u> to the door.

_____ **2.** Don't <u>panic</u>! We've got to think!

_____ **3.** Everyone is sure to <u>gossip</u> about the new girl.

_____ **4.** The police detective found signs of a <u>struggle</u>.

_____ **5.** Don't believe that story; it's just <u>gossip</u>.

_____ **6.** The dealer <u>shuffled</u> the playing cards.

_____ **7.** There was <u>panic</u> in her eyes.

_____ **8.** I have to <u>struggle</u> to get out of bed in the morning.

❧ Chapter Two: Part Two ❧

(pages 29–37)

BEFORE YOU READ

Take a look at the following words and expressions.

PAGE

29   **take a sock at you** = try to hit you

        we're gonna get the can = we're going to get fired, lose our jobs

30   **let 'im have it** = hit him hard

31   **heavily made up** = wearing lots of cosmetics

        mules = high-heeled slippers or shoes that are open in the back

32   **a tramp** = an immoral woman, especially a prostitute

        clear out = run away, leave

        jail bait = a girl younger than the legal age for sex (A man can go to jail for having sex with her.)

33   **pan gold** = look for gold in the sand and rocks of a river bottom

        mules = animals that are a cross between a horse and a donkey

35   **bitch** = female dog

        She slang her pups = She gave birth to a litter of puppies

ON YOUR OWN

Reading

Read the rest of Chapter 2 *without stopping*.

Try to get the main idea of what is happening in the story without pausing at new words.

A Closer Look

1. What have you learned about these characters so far?

    Curley's wife

    Slim

    Carlson

2. How does Lennie feel about being in this place?

3. Who is Lulu?

4. What idea does Carlson suggest to Slim?

5. What is Lennie excited about?

Write any questions *you* have about this chapter.

DISCUSSION

1. After Curley's wife leaves, George says, "Curley got his work ahead of him" (32). What does he mean?

2. What do you think about Carlson and his idea for solving the problem of Candy's dog? What other possible solutions can you think of?

3. Rank the following characters in order of their importance on the ranch. Make a list starting with the person you think has the highest status and going down to the person with the lowest status.

George, Lennie, Candy (the old swamper), the boss, the stable buck, Curley, Curley's wife, Slim, Carlson

4. If you are keeping a reading journal, share something you have written. Read aloud what you noticed in the novel—what you wrote on the left side of your journal page—and tell why it made an impression on you. Explain your thoughts about it.

SUGGESTIONS FOR WRITING

Personal Response

Make an entry in your reading journal.

Summarizing

Sometimes we use the *present* tense in writing a summary. With present tense verbs, the summary sounds as if the action is happening now. That is fine because a story happens again every time someone new comes to the novel and reads it.

Activity 1   Write the verbs in this summary in the simple present tense.

George and Lennie ___*arrive*___ at the ranch the next
(arrive)

morning. An old man with one hand _____ them to the bunk
(show)

house. The boss _____ in and _____ them, and he
(come)   (question)

_____ George of taking advantage of Lennie. Next they
(suspect)

_____the boss's son, Curley, a small man who _____
(meet)   (look)

Lennie over, sizing him up for a fight. After Curley _____,
(leave)

George _____ Lennie again to go to the river to hide if he
(tell)

_____ into trouble. From the old swamper, they _____
(get)   (hear)

that Curley's pretty new wife _____ too much interest in
(show)

other men. When this woman_____ at the door, Lennie
(appear)

_____ her, fascinated. Two other ranch hands, Slim and
(watch)

Carlson, _____, and Lennie _____ excited to learn
(arrive)   (be)

that Slim's dog Lulu has just had puppies.

Sometimes we use the *past* tense in writing a summary. Then the summary sounds as if the story has already happened. That is fine, too.

Activity 2   Write the verbs in this summary in the simple past tense.

The following morning, George and Lennie ___*got*___ to the (get)

ranch. An old ranch worker with one hand missing _____ (take)

them to the bunk house, where they _____ the boss. He (meet)

_____ suspicious because George _____ all the (be)   (do)

talking for Lennie. They also _____ a tense meeting with (have)

the boss's son, Curley, a small man ready for a fight. George

_____ Lennie to stay away from him. The old man _____ (warn)   (gossip)

to George about Curley's pretty new wife and _____ her "a (call)

tramp." When she _____ in for a minute, Lennie_____ (stop)   (stare)

at her in fascination. Two more ranch hands _____ in, (come)

Slim and Carlson, and Lennie _____ that Slim's dog, Lulu, (find out)

had puppies. Carlson _____ giving one to Candy to replace (suggest)

his smelly old dog.

❧

When *you* write a summary, you can use present or past, but choose one and be consistent.

Points of Departure

1. When George and Lennie meet their new boss, he treats them with suspicion. Have you ever gone into a new situation and felt that you had to prove yourself? Have you ever felt that someone was skeptical of your abilities or that they did not trust you? Describe the situation: tell how you felt, how you reacted to the situation, and what happened.

2. This chapter of the novel begins with a detailed description of the inside of the bunk house. Think of a room that you know well: it could be where you live now, or a room where you study, or a room you remember from your childhood. Close your eyes and look around that room slowly. What things do you see? What kind of a place is it? How do you feel about it? Write about it in detail so that your readers can see it, too.

3. On pages 33–34, the author describes Slim, what he looks like, how he moves, what he can do, and what other people think of him. Write a description of someone you know, perhaps someone you admire. Include a physical description, with details about how this person looks, dresses, moves, sounds. What is this person good at? How do others react to him or her? How do you feel about this person?

WORDS TO KNOW

* = irregular verb

PAGE

31   **brusquely** *(adv.)* George didn't want to be drawn into conversation with Curley's wife, so he spoke **brusquely** to her.

        fascinated *(adj.)* Lennie stared at the girl in the doorway, **fascinated** by her.

32   **apprehensive** *(adj.)* When she heard Curley was at their house, Curley's wife became **apprehensive** and quickly left.

33   **authority** *(n.)* Slim had such great **authority** among the men that they accepted his opinion on any subject.

34   **compliment** *(n.)* George told Slim how strong Lennie was, and Lennie smiled with pleasure at the **compliment**.

       confidence *(n.)* Slim's friendly manner invited **confidences**.

35   **drown** *(v.)* Slim **drowned** four of the puppies because there were too many for Lulu to feed.

36   **stink** *(v.)** Carlson complained about the smell of Candy's dog. He said the dog **stank**.

       dignity *(n.)* When Slim stood up, he moved slowly, with **dignity**.

       precede *(v.)* Carlson waited and let Slim **precede** him through the door and out of the bunk house.

37   **insultingly** *(adv.)* George didn't try to be polite to Curley. He answered him **insultingly**.

Exercise 1   Write each word next to its definition.

authority   **a compliment**   **dignity**

1. _____ power to influence others

2. _____ a calm, serious, formal attitude

3. _____ an expression of praise or admiration

Exercise 2   Use one of the following words to complete each sentence about the story. Change word forms as needed.

apprehensive brusquely drown fascinated insultingly precede

1.   George didn't want to get into conversation with Curley's wife, so he answered her _____, with few words.

2.   Lennie stared at the girl in the doorway. He was _____ by her.

3.   Curley's wife became _____ when she heard that her husband had gone into their house. She was afraid of something.

4.   Slim reported that he _____ the smallest four of Lulu's puppies because nine were too many for her to feed.

5.   Carlson stood back to let Slim _____ him through the door and then followed him out of the bunk house.

6.   George disliked Curley and didn't speak politely to him. In fact, he spoke _____.

Exercise 3 Use the same words to complete the following sentences, which are *not* related to the story. Change word forms as needed.

apprehensive   brusquely   drown fascinated   insultingly   precede

1.   The patient was very _____ when he went to see his doctor. He was afraid to learn the results of his tests.

2.　The fight started when one man spoke _____ about the other man's wife.

3.　Reporters waiting outside the courthouse shouted questions at the lawyer. He answered them _____ as he rushed by.

4.　Ronald Reagan _____ George Bush as President of the U.S. Reagan was in the White House from 1980 to 1988 and then Bush from 1988 to 1992.

5.　The children were _____ by the fish in the aquarium and watched them for a long time.

6.　Two swimmers were swept out to sea by a strong current and _____ before lifeguards could reach them.

NOUNS	VERBS	ADJECTIVES	ADVERBS
_____	_____	fascinated fascinating	

Exercise 4　Use your dictionary to complete the chart above. Then fill in each blank with the appropriate member of this word family.

1.　The girl standing in the doorway was a _____ sight.

2.　Lennie was _____ by her. He couldn't take his eyes off her.

NOUNS	VERBS	ADJECTIVES	ADVERBS
_____	_____	_____ _____	insultingly

Exercise 5 Use your dictionary to complete the chart above. Then fill in each blank with the appropriate member of this word family.

1. George made an _____ remark to Curley.

2. Do you think Curley felt _____ when George made a remark about his wife?

---

confidence

a. *(n.)* belief or trust in one's own ability or in another person

b. *(n.)* something personal told to someone in private, a secret

c. **in confidence**: in private, as a secret

Exercise 6 Look at the box above. Which meaning does "confidence" have in each of the following sentences? Write the letter of the definition next to each sentence.

_____ **1.** I can't tell you what she said because she spoke to me in **confidence**.

_____ **2.** I'm sure you'll do an excellent job. I have great **confidence** in you.

_____ **3.** Slim's way of acting and speaking invited **confidences** from other men.

TEST YOURSELF

VOCABULARY REVIEW FOR CHAPTER 1, PARTS 1 AND 2

1. Are the underlined words in these pairs of sentences similar or different in meaning? Circle the letters of the pairs that are similar.

   a. They <u>emerged from</u> the room.

   They <u>came out of</u> the room.

   b. He <u>grinned</u> at me.

   He <u>scowled</u> at me.

   c. Would you <u>look after</u> my cat?

   Would you <u>follow</u> my cat?

   d. She looked <u>ashamed</u>.

   She looked <u>embarrassed</u>.

   e. He <u>imitated</u> the teacher.

   He <u>reminded</u> the teacher.

   f. She's <u>reluctant</u> to do it.

   She's <u>ready</u> to do it.

   g. Who's <u>tending</u> the campfire?

   Who's <u>taking care of</u> the campfire?

2. Use the clues given below to fill in the words in the puzzle.

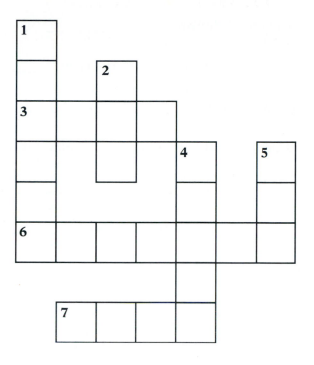

ACROSS

3. unkind, cruel, causing hurt

6. feeling of strong dislike or impatience

7. a rough track or trail

DOWN

1. to make (someone) remember

2. the foot of an animal with claws or nails

4. bushes, plants, and low trees

5. an animal kept in the house

All the words in the puzzle appear in this list:

brush	grin	pet
cave	imitate	remind
denim	mean	scowl
disgust	path	stroke
emerge	paw	tend

3. Answer the following questions about the story.

    a. What was made of **denim**? _____

    b. Who sat and stared **morosely** into the river? _____

    c. What was Lennie **stroking**? _____

    d. When did George and Lennie have to "**sneak** out in the dark"?

    _____

    e. Who talked about going to live in a **cave**? _____

    f. What did Lennie have **by heart**? _____

❧ Chapter Three: Part One ❧

(pages 38–50)

BEFORE YOU READ

Take a look at the following words and expressions.

PAGE

38   **a horseshoe game** = a game in which players throw horseshoes, aiming for a metal stake in the ground

        It wasn't much to you = It wasn't important to you

39   **hands** = workers

        Never seem to give a damn = [The men] never seem to care

40   **Clean forgot** = [Lennie] completely forgot

        a nice fella = a nice guy

41   **I ain't got no people** = I have no family

        the girl lets out a squawk = the girl screams

        scairt = scared

43   **the nest** = the "bed" the mother dog prepared for her puppies

45   **Carlson was not to be put off.** = Carlson refused to give up.

        a cripple = a person disabled by injury or since birth (This word can be offensive.)

46   **a pulp magazine** = a cheap popular magazine

        he is a whing-ding = he is great

47   **I'll put the old devil out of his misery** = I'll kill the dog to end his suffering and pain

        a Luger = a type of handgun

50   **turning his hand** = working

stick aroun' = stay

negro = African-American, black (The word "Negro" was commonly used in Steinbeck's time but can be offensive now.)

ON YOUR OWN

Reading

Read pages 38–50 *without stopping.*

Read for the main idea of what is happening in the story. Try not to pause for new words.

A Closer Look

1.   As this chapter opens, what time is it?

2.   What has Slim given to Lennie? Is this a good idea? Why or why not?

3.   What does Lennie try to hide from George?

4. What is Slim's opinion of Lennie? Find three comments Slim makes about Lennie that show what Slim thinks of him.

5. Why does Candy agree to let Carlson shoot his dog? Give at least two reasons.

Write any questions *you* have about this chapter so far.

SCENE FROM THE NOVEL

The following scene is excerpted from *Of Mice and Men: A Play in Three Acts* by John Steinbeck (New York: The Viking Press, 1937), pages 77–81. You will need three people to read aloud the parts of Slim, George, and Lennie. Before reading aloud, practice your role by reading your lines softly to yourself.

This scene takes place on Friday evening. George and Slim are seated on opposite sides of the table in the bunk house. Slim is braiding a whip, while George is picking up the playing cards scattered across the table. They have been talking about George and Lennie's friendship.

SLIM: [Lennie's] a nice fella. A guy don't need no sense to be a nice fella. Seems to be sometimes it's jest the other way round. Take a real smart guy, he ain't hardly ever a nice fella.

GEORGE: *stacking the scattered cards and getting his solitaire game ready again:* I ain't got no people. I seen guys that go round on the ranches alone. That ain't no good. They don't have no fun. After a while they get mean.

SLIM: *quietly:* Yeah, I seen 'em get mean. I seen 'em get so they don't want to talk to nobody. Some ways they got to. You take a bunch of guys all livin' in one room an' by God they got to mind their own business. 'Bout the only private thing a guy's got is where he come from and where he's goin'.

GEORGE: 'Course Lennie's a goddamn nuisance most of the time. But you get used to goin' round with a guy and you can't get rid of him. I mean you get used to him an' you can't get rid of bein' used to him. I'm sure drippin' at the mouth. I ain't told nobody all this before.

SLIM: Do you want to git rid of him?

GEORGE: Well, he gets in trouble all the time. Because he's so goddamn dumb. Like what happened in Weed. *He stops, alarmed at what he has said.* You wouldn't tell nobody?

SLIM: *calmly:* What did he do in Weed?

GEORGE: You wouldn't tell?—No, course you wouldn't.

SLIM: What did he do?

GEORGE: Well, he seen this girl in a red dress. Dumb bastard like he is he wants to touch everything he likes. Jest wants to feel of it. So he reaches out to feel this red dress. Girl lets out a squawk and that gets Lennie all mixed up. He holds on 'cause that's the only thing he can think to do.

SLIM: The hell!

GEORGE: Well, this girl squawks her head off. I'm right close and I hear all the yellin', so I comes a-running. By that time Lennie's scared to death. You know, I had to sock him over the head with a fence picket to make him let go.

SLIM: So what happens then?

GEORGE: *carefully building his solitaire hand:* Well, she runs in and tells the law she's been raped. The guys in Weed start out to lynch Lennie. So there we sit in an irrigation ditch, under water all the rest of that day. Got only our heads sticking out of water, up under the grass that grows out of the side of the ditch. That night we run outa there.

SLIM: Didn't hurt the girl none, huh?

GEORGE: Hell no, he jes' scared her.

SLIM: He's a funny guy.

GEORGE: Funny! Why, one time, you know what that big baby done! He was walking along a road—*Enter Lennie through the door. He wears his coat over his shoulder like a cape and walks hunched over.* Hi, Lennie. How do you like your pup?

LENNIE: *breathlessly:* He's brown and white jus' like I wanted. *Goes directly to his bunk and lies down. Face to the wall and knees drawn up.*

GEORGE: *puts down his cards deliberately:* Lennie!

LENNIE: *over his shoulder:* Huh? What you want George?

GEORGE: *sternly:* I tole ya, ya couldn't bring that pup in here.

LENNIE: What pup, George? I ain't got no pup. *George goes quickly over to him, grabs him by the shoulder and rolls him over. He picks up a tiny puppy from where Lennie has been concealing it against his stomach.*

LENNIE: *quickly:* Give him to me, George.

GEORGE: You get right up and take this pup to the nest. He's got to sleep with his mother. Ya want ta kill him? Jes' born last night and ya take him out of the nest. Ya take him back or I'll tell Slim not to let you have him.

LENNIE: *pleadingly:* Give him to me, George. I'll take him back. I didn't mean no bad thing, George. Honest I didn't. I jus' want to pet him a little.

GEORGE: *giving the pup to him:* All right, you get him back there quick. And don't you take him out no more.

LENNIE: *scuttles out of the room.*

SLIM: Jesus, he's just like a kid, ain't he?

DISCUSSION

1. Should George and Lennie have stayed in Weed and explained to the people what really happened with the girl? Why or why not?

2. How did George and Lennie's friendship begin?

3. How has George's treatment of Lennie changed?

4. Why does Candy let Carlson shoot his dog? List as many reasons as you can.

5. Was shooting Candy's dog the best thing to do? Why or why not?

WORDS TO KNOW

* = irregular verb

PAGE

38 **a barn** *(n.)* George knew that Lennie would want to sleep in the **barn** near his puppy.

39 **keep up with** *(v.)** Lennie was so strong and worked so hard that nobody could **keep up with** him.

defensively *(adv.)* George reacted **defensively** to Slim's remark that his friendship with Lennie was "funny."

a crop *(n.)* George said if he were smart, he would have his own land and be bringing in **crops** of his own.

41 **a nuisance** *(n.)* George said that Lennie was usually "a God damn **nuisance**."

42 **rape** *(v.)* The girl ran into town and reported that she had been **raped**.

lynch *(v.)* A group of men from Weed set out to find Lennie and **lynch** him.

43 **conceal** *(v.)* Lennie **concealed** the puppy against his stomach, but he didn't fool George.

harm *(n.)* Lennie didn't think he was hurting the puppy. He told George he meant no **harm**.

44 **apologize** *(v.)* Candy **apologized** for the way his dog smelled.

can't stand *(v.)* Carlson told Candy that he **couldn't stand** having the dog in they bunk house.

stiff *(adj.)* Carlson pointed out that the dog had no teeth and was **stiff** with rheumatism.

45 **kind** *(adj.)* According to Carlson, it wasn't **kind** of Candy to keep the dog alive.

47 **uneasily** *(adv.)* Candy watched Carlson **uneasily**, afraid of what Carlson might do.

get (something) **over with** *(v.)** Carlson said he would shoot the dog right away and **get it over with**.

49 **still** *(adv.)* On his bunk, the old man lay **still** and silently stared up at the ceiling.

Exercise 1 Write each word on the line next to its definition.

a barn   a crop   lynch   rape

1. _____ grain, fruit, or vegetables grown by a farmer

2. _____ attack (with a crowd of people) and kill—especially by hanging—someone accused of a crime

3. _____ a farm building for storing crops or housing farm animals

4. _____ force a person to have sex

Exercise 2 Use one of the following words or phrases to complete each sentence about the story. Change word forms as needed.

conceal   defensively   get it over with   keep up with
nuisance   uneasily

1. Slim was impressed by how much work Lennie could do. Lennie's partner couldn't do so much. In fact, no one could _____ Lennie.

2. George felt that he was under attack when Slim commented that his friendship with Lennie was strange. George reacted _____, asking, "What's funny about it?" (39)

3. Because Lennie caused a lot of trouble for George, George called him a _____.

4. Lennie held his puppy under his jacket to _____ it from George.

5. Candy was afraid of what Carlson might do, so he watched Carlson _____.

6. Carlson didn't want to wait until the next day to shoot Candy's dog. He wanted to _____ right away.

Exercise 3 Use the same words and phrases in the following sentences, which are *not* related to the story. Make changes in word forms as needed.

**conceal   defensively   get it over with   keep up with
nuisance   uneasily**

1. Airports have X-ray machines to check passengers' bags, to make sure no one _____ a weapon.

2. The runner from Jamaica won the race easily. Nobody could _____ her.

3. Let's do the work first thing in the morning and _____. Then we won't have to worry about it.

4. It makes sense to drive _____, making sure you are on guard against careless drivers.

5. Some people say that having a car in the city is a _____, not a convenience.

6. As we began our picnic lunch on the grass, we looked up _____ at the heavy dark clouds gathering in the sky.

Exercise 4 Draw a line from each word or phrase to its opposite.

1. can't stand   a. help, improve

2. harm   b. mean, cruel

3. kind   c. flexible, loose

4. stiff   d. enjoy, love

NOUNS	VERBS	ADJECTIVES	ADVERBS
_____	apologize	_____	_____

Exercise 5   Use your dictionary to complete the chart above. Then fill in each blank with the appropriate member of this word family.

1. Candy _____ for the way his dog smelled.

2. He spoke _____ to Carlson.

3. Candy was _____ about the bad smell from his dog.

4. Candy's _____ didn't satisfy Carlson.

> **still**
>
> a. *(adv.)* motionless
> b. *(adv.)* until a certain time, yet
> c. *(adv.)* all the same, nevertheless
>   From *The Newbury House Dictionary of American English*

Exercise 6   Look at the box above. Which meaning does "still" have in each of the following sentences? Write the letter of the definition next to each sentence.

_____ **1.** It's almost noon and he is **still** in bed!

_____ **2.** She didn't study, but she **still** passed the exam.

_____ **3.** You have to sit **still** for your haircut.

Chapter Three: Part Two

(pages 50–65)

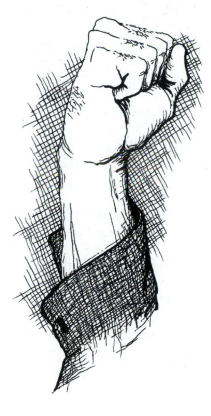

BEFORE YOU READ

Take a look at the following words and expressions.

PAGE

52 **What's it set you back?** = What does it cost you?

a shot = a small amount of whiskey

clean = free of sexually transmitted diseases

53 **bucks** = dollars

What's eating on Curley? = What is bothering Curley?

54 **spoilin'** = eager for a fight

get mixed up in = get involved in

56 **You give me a good whore house every time** = I would rather pay for sex with a prostitute than get involved with girls like Curley's wife.

how much it's gonna set him back = how much it will cost him and what the consequences will be

These here jail baits is just set on the trigger of the hoosegow. = Young girls will get you into trouble that will send you to jail.

San Quentin = a prison in California

on account of = because of

59 **flat bust** = without any money

kick off = die

60 **we could swing her** = we could manage to get the place

they'll put me on the county = they'll put me in a public institution for poor old people

61 **They li 'ble to can us** = They would probably fire us

62 **step outside** = go outdoors and fight

    yella = "yellow," cowardly, afraid

64 **This punk sure had it comin' to him.** = This troublemaker certainly deserved punishment for the way he behaved.

ON YOUR OWN

Reading

Read the rest of the chapter *without stopping*.

A Closer Look

1. What do the ranch hands usually do on Saturday nights?

2. What offer does Candy make to George and Lennie?

3. What do you think of Candy's offer?

4. What does Candy say to George about letting Carlson shoot his dog?

5. Do you agree with what Candy says? Why or why not?

6. What happens when Curley gets into a fight with Lennie?

Write any questions *you* have about this chapter.

DISCUSSION

1. Why does George say, "You give me a good whore house every time" (56)?

2. For Lennie, the rabbits are the most important part of the plan for a place of their own. What do you think is most important to George? Why?

3. Why does Slim say to Curley, "I think you got your han' caught in a machine" (64)?

4. Do you think Curley will keep quiet about what really happened? Why or why not?

5. Look back at the questions and predictions you wrote earlier. (See page 38 of the *Companion.*) Can you answer any of your questions? Have any of your predictions come true? Do you have anything to add?

SUGGESTIONS FOR WRITING

Personal Response

Make an entry in your reading journal.

Summarizing

Activity 1 Write a summary of this chapter. You can begin this way:

The third chapter of *Of Mice and Men* takes place in the bunk house on the evening of George and Lennie's first day on the ranch.

Your summary should contain the answers to the following questions:

What has Slim given to Lennie?

What does George talk about with Slim?

What does Carlson pressure Candy to do?

What happens to Candy's dog?

What does George hear from Whit?

What happens when Candy overhears George telling Lennie about a little ranch that is for sale?

What happens when Curley comes in?

Activity 2 Complete this chart of events in the novel so far.

Chapter	When	Where	What happens
1	Thursday evening	by the river	George and Lennie camp. They talk about work on the ranch and their plan for land of their own.
2	Friday morning	bunk house	
3			

Points of Departure

1. George and Lennie have been on the ranch just one day, but a great deal has happened. What do you think they should do now? Write what you would advise them to do and why.

2. Have you ever been in a fight or watched a fight take place? Describe the situation: What led to the fight? What happened during the fight? What resulted from the fight? How did you feel about it at that time, and how do you feel about it now?

3. George confided in Slim about how his friendship with Lennie had changed. Over time, relationships often change. Sometimes we learn to appreciate someone in ways that we didn't before; sometimes we lose faith in someone we used to trust; and sometimes our feelings about a person take us by surprise. Write about a relationship in your life—with a friend, an acquaintance, or a family member—in which you experienced a change. How did this relationship begin? How did it change? What place does this relationship have in your life now?

WORDS TO KNOW

* = irregular verb

PAGE

51 **casually** *(adv.)* George spoke **casually** when he asked if Curley's new wife had been any trouble on the ranch.

show up *(v.)** Whit told George that Curley's wife always **showed up** when the men were around.

53 **threateningly** *(adv.)* Curley asked the men if they had seen his wife and then looked around **threateningly**.

56 **sigh** *(v.)* After questioning Lennie closely, George **sighed**.

an acre *(n.)* George knew of a place with ten **acres** of land that they could buy.

58 **subside** *(v.)* Lennie's anger **subsided**, but he went on muttering to himself.

entranced *(adj.)* George was **entranced**, imagining the life they would lead if they had a place of their own.

59   **eagerly** *(adv.)* Candy leaned forward **eagerly** and made his offer.

a will *(n.)* Candy said he would make a **will** leaving his share of the place to George and Lennie.

60   **miserably** *(adv.)* The old man spoke **miserably** about what had happened to his dog.

62   **rage** *(n.)* Curley exploded with **rage** and attacked Lennie.

63   **retreat** *(v.)* Lennie didn't want to fight, so he tried to **retreat**.

a fist *(n.)* Lennie caught Curley's **fist** in his big hand.

64   **crouch** *(v.)* When the fight was over, Lennie **crouched** against the wall, miserable and afraid.

fault *(n.)* Slim reassured Lennie, saying the fight hadn't been Lennie's **fault**.

65   **bruise** *(v.)* After the fight, Lennie had a **bruised** mouth.

Exercise 1 Write each word next to its definition.

an acre   **bruise**   **retreat**   **sigh**

1. _____ injure without breaking the skin

2. _____ about 4,050 square meters of land

3. _____ move back (away from danger or difficulty)

4. _____ slowly let out a deep breath, often to express an emotion such as sadness, tiredness, or pleasure

Exercise 2 Use one of the following words or phrases to complete each sentence about the story. Change word forms as needed.

crouch   **fault**   **fist**   **rage**   **show up**   **subside**

1. Whit said that Curley's wife always appeared at the bunk house whenever the men were there. "Ever' time the guys is around she _____."

2. Lennie got very upset thinking about cats hurting his rabbits, but then he calmed down. His anger _____.

3. Curley was angry with his wife and with Slim, Carlson, and Candy, too. All this _____ inside Curley exploded when he saw Lennie smiling.

4. Curley tried to hit Lennie, but Lennie caught his _____ and held it.

5. After Lennie let go of Curley, he _____ by the wall, miserable and afraid.

6. Slim didn't blame Lennie for hurting Curley because Curley started the fight. Slim said it wasn't Lennie's _____.

Exercise 3   Use the same words and phrases in the following sentences, which are *not* related to the story. Change word forms as needed.

crouch   fault   fist   rage   show up   subside

1. The photographer _____ down to take a picture of some little flowers.

2. The teenager said, "They promised to come to my party. I'll be mad if they don't _____."

3. The storm brought strong winds which _____ after a couple of hours.

4. The taxi driver was furious at the man driving the car that hit his taxi. The taxi driver yelled at the man in _____.

5. The other driver yelled back, "What are you yelling at me for? This was all your _____!"

6. The taxi driver raised his arm and shook his _____ at the other man.

Exercise 4   Are the underlined words in these pairs of sentences similar or different in meaning? Write your answers in the spaces.

1. He spoke <u>casually</u>.

    He spoke <u>carefully</u>.   _____

2. They began <u>eagerly</u>.

    They began <u>reluctantly</u>.   _____

3. She was <u>entranced</u>.

    She was <u>fascinated</u>.   _____

4. We waited <u>miserably</u>.

    We waited <u>happily</u>.   _____

NOUNS	VERBS	ADJECTIVES	ADVERBS
_____	_____	_____	threateningly

Exercise 5   Use your dictionary to complete the chart above. Then fill in each blank with the appropriate member of this word family.

1.   Curley stared _____ at Lennie.

2.   There was a _____ expression on Curley's face.

3.   Lennie could see the _____ in Curley's look.

4.   Curley _____ Lennie. He said that Lennie had better answer when Curley spoke to him.

---

will

a. *(n.)* the strength of the mind to control one's actions, *(syn.)* determination

b. *(n.)* power to decide

c. *(n.)* a legal document that tells who will receive [someone's] money and property when that person dies

From *The Newbury House Dictionary of American English*

Exercise 6   Look at the box above. Which meaning does "will" have in each of the following sentences? Write the letter of the definition next to each sentence.

_____   1.   She went to the police and confessed of her own free **will**; no one made her do it.

_____   2.   The patient was in serious condition, but he had a great **will** to live and refused to give up hope.

_____   3.   Candy offered to write a **will** leaving his share of the place to George and Lennie.

TEST YOURSELF

VOCABULARY REVIEW FOR CHAPTER 2, PARTS 1 AND 2

1. Choose the phrase from the list below that best completes each statement, and write it in the space provided.

   . . . stared at him.
   . . . reassured him.
   . . . fascinated him.
   .✓. made him panic.
   . . . complimented him.
   . . . preceded him out of the bunk house.

   a. When Lennie had to answer the boss's question, it _made_
   him panic.

   b. George calmed down after hearing the old swamper's
   explanation. It _____

   c. Lennie squirmed uncomfortably when Curley _____

   d. The pretty girl in the doorway interested Lennie. In fact, she

   _____

   e. Lennie heard George tell Slim how strong he was. He smiled
   when George_____

f. As a gesture of respect, Carlson stepped back, and Slim

_____

2. Unscramble these words. (Their definitions follow in parentheses.)

a. wondr = _ _ _ _ _ (die under water because unable to breathe)

b. rockoed = _ _ _ _ _ _ _ (not straight)

c. fleuhfs = _ _ _ _ _ _ _ (walk slowly without lifting one's feet)

d. gluesrtg = _ _ _ _ _ _ _ _ (make a strong effort, fight)

e. tthroauiy = _ _ _ _ _ _ _ _ _ (ability and power to influence or control)

3. Answer these questions about the story.

a. Who warns George he can't **get away with** anything? _____

b. Who **shows off**? _____

c. Who **gossips** about Curley's wife? _____

d. Who gives Lennie a **calculating** look? _____

e. Who speaks **brusquely** to Curley's wife? _____

f. Who feels **apprehensive**? _____

4. Find and circle the words in this puzzle that are defined below. Words are written going down, across from left to right, or diagonally from left to right. Write each word you find next to its definition.

```
D  I  G  N  I  T  Y  K  P  C
E  N  X  Q  S  B  Z  M  X  O
R  S  T  A  K  E  H  W  Q  N
O  U  T  P  E  S  C  O  F  F
G  L  B  L  P  W  X  Z  Q  I
A  T  Z  R  T  M  V  G  W  D
T  I  S  T  I  N  K  R  X  E
O  N  X  C  C  G  T  W  Q  N
R  G  L  W  A  Q  H  N  P  C
Y  G  I  L  L  Z  W  T  X  E
```

a. S C O F F = speak or laugh in a disrespectful way

b. _ _ _ _ _ = have a very bad smell

c. _ _ _ _ _ = an investment or interest, especially a financial one

d. _ _ _ _ _ _ = smart, intelligent

e. _ _ _ _ _ _ _ _ = calm and serious manner of behaving

f. _ _ _ _ _ _ _ _ _ = offensive, hurtful to someone's feelings or pride

g. _ _ _ _ _ _ _ _ _ _ = doubting or disbelieving, distrustful

h. _ _ _ _ _ _ _ _ _ _ _ = showing contempt or a lack of respect

i. _ _ _ _ _ _ _ _ _ _ _ = something told in secret, or firm trust (in oneself or someone else)

❧ Chapter Four: Part One ❧

(pages 66–74)

BEFORE YOU READ

ON YOUR OWN

Reading

Read pages 66–74 *without stopping.*

A Closer Look

1. What day is it, and what time of day?

2. Why does Lennie come to Crooks' room?

3. Where have all the other ranch hands gone?

4. How does Crooks react to Lennie at first?

5. Why does Crooks start to enjoy talking to Lennie?

Write any questions *you* have about these pages.

DISCUSSION

1. How has Crooks suffered from racism?

2. On page 71, find:

    "Crooks' face lighted with pleasure in his torture."

    How is Crooks torturing Lennie? Why does this give Crooks pleasure?

3. Where do you see a shift in power and control from Crooks to Lennie?

4. Why is Crooks scornful when Lennie tells him about the plans that he, George, and Candy have? Choose the statement below that you think best answers this question:

    ____ Crooks knows Lennie isn't normal, and he thinks Lennie is just talking like a crazy person.

    ____ Crooks is bitter; he has no hope left in life and wants to crush anyone else's hopes.

    ____ Crooks is skeptical. Ranch hands always talk like this, but in his experience, no one ever gets any land.

    ____ Other:

    Explain your choice.

WORDS TO KNOW

72   **approach** *(v.)* As Lennie **approached** him, Crooks edged back in retreat.

74   **scornful** *(adj.)* Crooks was **scornful** of Lennie for believing that he and George would really get their own land.

heaven *(n.)* According to Crooks, nobody ever gets to **heaven**.

Exercise 1   Write each word next to its definition.

heaven   **torture**   **a victory**

1. _____ a win (in a war, struggle, or competition)

2. _____ severe pain inflicted on someone to get information, as punishment, or for pleasure

3. _____ a place of perfect happiness

Exercise 2   Use one of the following words to complete each sentence about the story. Change word forms as needed.

aloof   approach   bore   lean   scornful   suppose

1. Crooks was a proud man who kept to himself, holding himself _____ from the other men.

2. Crooks was a thin man with a _____ face.

3. The look from Crooks' eyes was so intense it seemed that he could _____ a hole through Lennie.

4. Talking to Lennie, Crooks asked him to _____ that George didn't come back: what would Lennie do then?

5. Lennie got up and _____ Crooks, demanding "Who

hurt George?" Crooks moved back, trying to get away.

6. When Lennie told Crooks about the plan for land of their own, Crooks was _____. He laughed at Lennie in an unpleasant way.

Exercise 3 Use the same words in the following sentences, which are *not* related to the story. Change word forms as needed.

aloof   approach   bore   lean   scornful   suppose

1. Workers from the oil company had to _____ through solid rock before they found oil.

2. _____ it rains tomorrow. If it does, what will we do about the picnic?

3. Long-distance runners are never fat; they're always _____.

4. Members of the opposition party were _____ of the plan announced by the president. They called it crazy.

5. I realized I was lost, so I _____ a police officer to ask for directions.

6. The professor wasn't friendly to students. He was _____ and difficult to approach.

NOUNS	VERBS	ADJECTIVES	ADVERBS
intensity	_____	_____	_____

Exercise 4 Use your dictionary to complete the chart above. Then fill in each blank with the appropriate member of this word family.

1. Crooks is a man of _____ feelings.

2. Lennie couldn't understand the _____ of Crooks' feelings.

3. Crooks _____ the pressure on Lennie by leaning forward
and repeating his question, "What'll ya do then?"

4. Crooks seems to be an _____ lonely man.

---

right

a. *(adj.)* correct, accurate, exact

b. *(n.)* permission to do [something] guaranteed by law

c. *(n.)* morally correct behavior, good conduct

d. *(n.)* a conservative political party or wing

From *The Newbury House Dictionary of American English*

Exercise 5   Look at the box above. Which meaning does "right" have in
each of the following sentences? Write the letter of the definition next to
each sentence.

_____   **1.** The **Right** is sure to win more seats in the legislature in
the next election.

_____   **2.** Are you familiar with the U.S. Bill of **Rights**? The first
one deals with freedom of speech.

_____   **3.** I'm not sure I had the **right** answer to the math problem.

_____   **4.** Does Lennie know **right** from wrong?

bore

a. *(v.)* to cut a hole in [something], *(syn.)* to drill
b. *(v.)* to make [someone] feel tired
c. *(v.) past tense of* BEAR [to suffer]

From *The Newbury House Dictionary of American English*

Exercise 6 Look at the box above. Which meaning does "bore" have in each of the following sentences? Write the letter of the definition next to each sentence.

_____ **1.** The lecture **bored** me so much I fell asleep.

_____ **2.** He **bore** the pain of his aching tooth in silence.

_____ **3.** It seemed that Crooks could **bore** right through Lennie with the intensity of his eyes.

Chapter Four: Part Two

(pages 74–83)

BEFORE YOU READ

ON YOUR OWN

Reading

Read the rest of this chapter *without stopping*.

A Closer Look

1. How does Crooks feel about Candy coming into his room?

2. What offer does Crooks make to Candy?

3. What reason does Curley's wife give for coming to the barn?

4. What do you think she is really looking for?

5. Why does Curley's wife laugh and say to Lennie, "O.K., Machine. I'll talk to you later. I like machines."?

6. How does Curley's wife threaten Crooks?

7. What kind of person is Curley's wife? Choose the phrase you think best completes this statement:

Curley's wife is someone who is . . .

_____ mean, ambitious, and accustomed to using other people to get her own way.

_____ childish, thoughtless, and anxious to be the center of attention.

_____ lonely, disappointed, and trapped in a bad situation.

_____ Other:

Be ready to explain your opinion.

Write any questions *you* have about this chapter.

SCENE FROM THE NOVEL

Create a script for reading aloud part of the conversation that takes place in Crooks' room. You will need four people to read aloud the parts of Curley's wife, Candy, Crooks, and Lennie.

Turn to page 76 in the novel. Beginning with the last line on the page—"Any you boys seen Curley?"—underline the words each character speaks, and write the character's name in the margin. Continue through the line on page 80 where Curley's wife says, "I like machines." Here is an example:

Curley's wife   "Any you boys seen Curley?"

They swung their heads toward the door. Looking in was Curley's wife. Her face was heavily made up. Her lips were slightly parted. She breathed strongly, as though she had been running.

Candy   "Curley ain't been here," Candy said sourly.

(pages 76–77)

You can make changes in your part if you are uncomfortable speaking the dialect of the character. For example, you could change Candy's line to "Curley hasn't been here." Be careful not to change the meaning of a character's words.

Stage directions: Crooks is lying on his bunk looking toward the door of his room. Facing Crooks are Lennie, who is sitting to the right of the door, and Candy, who is standing to the left. They turn to look at Curley's wife when she steps into the doorway and speaks.

DISCUSSION

1. On page 77, Curley's wife says, "They left all the weak ones here." Tell how each one is "weak": Crooks, Lennie, Candy.

2. Is Curley's wife also weak? Why or why not?

3. In this chapter, find three times when someone is trying to exercise power over another person. Why do they do this?

4. What do you think of Curley's wife? Compare your answers to question 7 on page 98.

SUGGESTIONS FOR WRITING

Personal Response

Make an entry in your reading journal.

Summarizing

Write a summary of this chapter. It should be no more than 200 words long. Be sure to include when and where the action takes place. Who is there? Why are they there? What do they talk about? What new information comes out?

Points of Departure

1. Imagine that you are Crooks. Among the books on the shelf over your bunk is your diary. After the men leave your room, you take it down and write about the evening's events. In addition to describing what happened, write about how you felt.

2. Do you ever feel lonely? What do you do when you feel this way? Write about a time that you felt lonely. You might want to write about being alone and missing someone, or about being with other people but feeling that you are alone.

WORDS TO KNOW

* = irregular verb

80   **guiltily** *(adv.)* Lennie looked up **guiltily** when Curley's wife asked him about the bruises on his face.

81   **frame** *(v.)* Candy told Curley's wife that if she tried to **frame** Crooks, they would tell people the truth.

Exercise 1   Use one of the following words or phrases to complete each sentence about the story. Change word forms as needed.

get along   harvest   indignation   sullen   overwhelm

1.   Candy had always worked to plant and _____ crops for other people, never for himself, never on land of his own.

2.   The idea of a place of his own, with his own room and crops and animals, _____ Candy so that he couldn't speak.

3.   Curley's wife insisted that she _____ well with the men when she talked with them individually.

4.   At first Candy didn't dare to show his anger at Curley's wife openly, but his resentment was clear in the _____ way he spoke to her.

5.   The thought that everyone else was out having fun on Saturday night—while she was stuck talking to Crooks, Lennie, and Candy—filled Curley's wife with _____.

Exercise 2   Use the same words and phrases to complete the following sentences, which are *not* related to the story. Change word forms as needed.

get along   harvest   indignation   sullen   overwhelm

1.   The two brothers never speak to each other. They haven't _____ since they were children.

2. The students were _____ by the enormous amount of homework they had to do.

3. The children were promised a special treat for dessert, so when they were offered apples, they cried out in _____.

4. The workers didn't protest their boss's unfair treatment of them, but they did their jobs with _____ faces.

5. The American holiday of Thanksgiving began when the Pilgrims celebrated their first _____.

Exercise 3   Fill in each blank with one of these adverbs:

brutally   guiltily   irritably

1. Crooks invited Candy to come into his room, but he sounded annoyed. He spoke _____, as if he were in a bad mood.

2. Crooks didn't express his doubts in a kind or gentle way. He said _____, "You guys is just kiddin' yourself."

3. When Curley's wife asked Lennie about the bruises on his face, he looked up _____, feeling he had done a bad thing.

Exercise 4   Change the adverbs in Exercise 3 to *adjectives*. Use one in each of the following sentences, which are *not* related to the story.

1. A story about a _____ murder of two tourists was on the front page of today's newspaper.

2. The little girl told her mother that she hadn't touched the cookies, but she had a very _____ look on her face.

3. I'm sorry I spoke sharply to you. I have a headache, and that makes me _____.

> The adverb "irritably" is related to these three adjectives:
>
> irritable
> irritated
> irritating

Exercise 5   Look at the box above. Choose the appropriate word for each of the following sentences.

1.   Does Crooks seem to be an _____ person, someone who is easily annoyed or angered?

2.   Crooks spoke as if he were _____ with Candy for coming to his room.

3.   It wasn't really _____ for Crooks to have visitors: in truth, it was pleasing to him.

---

frame

a. *(n.)* a border placed around [something]

b. *(v.)* to put together, *(syn.)* to devise

c. *(v.)* to arrange the proof of a crime so that an innocent person appears guilty

From *The Newbury House Dictionary of American English*

Exercise 6   Look at the box above. Which meaning does "frame" have in each of the following sentences? Write the letter of the definition next to each sentence.

_____ **1.**   The interviewer had a sensitive question to ask, so she had to **frame** it carefully so as not to offend.

_____ **2.**   The photograph was in a lovely silver **frame**.

_____ **3.**   Curley's wife pointed out how easily she could **frame** Crooks for something he didn't do.

> **break in**
>
> a. *(v.)* to enter a building by force
>
> b. *(v.)* to interrupt
>
> c. *(v.)* to make [something] more comfortable
>
> From *The Newbury House Dictionary of American English*

Exercise 7   Look at the box above. Which meaning does "break in" have in each of the following sentences? Write the letter of the definition next to each sentence.

_____ **1.** After I've **broken in** my new shoes, they'll feel better.

_____ **2.** Someone **broke in** and stole their office computer last night.

_____ **3.** When Candy and Crooks were talking, Lennie **broke in** to ask about the rabbits.

TEST YOURSELF

VOCABULARY REVIEW FOR CHAPTER 3, PARTS 1 AND 2

1. Choose the word or phrase from the list below that best completes each statement, and write it in the space provided.

. . . retreat.
. . . stand it.
. . . show up.
. . . get it over with.
. . . keep up with him.

a. If the men were around, Curley's wife would always

_____

b. No one could work like Lennie; no one could

_____

c. Carlson didn't like the smell of Candy's dog. In fact, he couldn't

_____

d. Carlson urged Candy to let him shoot the dog right away, to

_____

e. Not wanting to fight Curley, Lennie tried to

_____

2. Are the underlined words in these pairs of sentences similar or different in meaning? Circle the letter of the pairs that are similar.

   a. He apologized to the girl.
       He threatened the girl.

   b. We were entranced.
       We were fascinated.

   c. She concealed the truth.
       She hid the truth.

   d. They raped someone.
       They lynched someone.

   e. He sat still as he waited.
       He squirmed as he waited.

   f. A little white lie won't do any harm.
       A little white lie won't do any damage.

3. Are the following statements true or false? Write "T" or "F."

   _____ a. People usually go to the dentist **eagerly**.

   _____ b. Thoughtful people speak **kindly** to someone who is upset.

   _____ c. Children tend to open presents **uneasily**.

   _____ d. Students usually take important exams **casually**.

   _____ e. A sick person might spend the day in bed **miserably**.

   _____ f. Puppies and kittens tend to move **stiffly**.

   _____ g. A person accused of a crime might react **defensively**.

4. Use the clues given below to fill in the words in this puzzle.

ACROSS

2. to calm down, to become quiet or less intense

4. someone or something that causes trouble or annoyance

6. the hand closed with fingers bent into the palm

7. a mistake, or the responsibility for some wrongdoing

8. to let out a breath to express tiredness, pleasure, etc.

DOWN

1. intense anger

3. to injure without breaking the skin

5. to lower one's body with knees bent

All of the words in the puzzle can be found in this list.

acre	conceal	fist	sigh
apology	crouch	misery	subside
barn	defend	nuisance	threaten
bruise	fault	rage	will

✺ Chapter Five ✺

(pages 84–98)

BEFORE YOU READ

ON YOUR OWN

Reading

Read the chapter *without stopping.*

A Closer Look

1. What has happened to Lennie's puppy?

2. What does Curley's wife confide to Lennie?

3. Describe what happens to her and how it happens.

4. What does Lennie decide to do then?

5. What happens when Candy brings the men into the barn?

6. What is George doing when he tells the men that Lennie would have gone south?

7. Carlson claims Lennie has stolen his gun. Do you think Lennie has the gun? Why or why not?

Write any questions *you* have about this chapter.

DISCUSSION

1. Do you agree or disagree with the following statement:

   Curley's wife is trying to seduce Lennie; she wants him to make love to her.

   Give reasons for your answers.

2. What possibilities do George, Candy, and Slim mention when they talk about what could happen to Lennie?

3. Considering all the possibilities mentioned in question 2, what would you do if you were George?

4. How much responsibility does each of the following people have for the killing:

   Lennie, Curley's wife, Curley, George

5. Why don't the boss, Candy's dog, and Curley's wife have names?

SUGGESTIONS FOR WRITING

Personal Response

Make an entry in your reading journal.

Summarizing

Write a summary of this chapter. It should be 100 to 200 words long.

Points of Departure

1. Write a biography of Curley's wife. Use your imagination to add to the information you have about her from the novel. For example:

What we know	What you might imagine
This story takes place in the mid-1930's. She went to live in Salinas as a child and grew up there with her mother (page 88.)	Curley's wife is about 20 years old and was born in 1915. (What about her father? Any brothers or sisters?)

In your biography, be sure to give her a name. Include how she came to live on the ranch, a description of her life there, and an account of her death.

2. When you look to the future, do you have plans? Do you have a dream? Do you have both plans and dreams? If so, how are they different? Write about your goals and desires and about what it will take for you to realize them.

WORDS TO KNOW

* = irregular verb

PAGE

85   **bounce** *(v.)* Lennie didn't think that he had **bounced** the puppy hard.

   inspect *(v.)* He uncovered the puppy, **inspected** it, and began to stroke it.

rock *(v.)* Feeling miserable, Lennie sat and **rocked** himself back and forth.

sorrow *(n.)* He was filled with **sorrow** over the puppy's death.

86 **kneel** *(v.)** Curley's wife **knelt** next to Lennie in the hay.

87 **console** *(v.)* She **consoled** Lennie, telling him not to worry.

88 **impress** *(v.)* Curley's wife thought Lennie would be **impressed** by her connection with Hollywood.

89 **confide** *(v.)* After **confiding** in Lennie, Curley's wife moved in closer to him and sat next to him.

90 **chuckle** *(v.)* Recalling the feel of velvet made Lennie **chuckle** with pleasure.

91 **muffle** *(v.)* Lennie's hand **muffled** the girl's screams.

bewildered *(adj.)* At first Lennie seemed **bewildered** at what had happened.

92 **creep** *(v.)** Lennie hid the puppy under his coat and **crept** to the wall of the barn.

discontent *(n.)* Death had erased from the girl's face all "the meanness and the plannings and the **discontent** and the ache for attention. . . ."

94   **echo** *(v.)* When he saw the body, George "**echoed** Candy's words. 'Oh, Jesus Christ!' "

starve *(v.)* George was sure that Lennie would **starve** if he got away and had to look after himself.

Exercise 1   Write each word next to its definition.

a chuckle   discontent   an echo   sorrow

1. _____ sadness, grief

2. _____ a quiet laugh

3. _____ unhappiness, dissatisfaction

4. _____ repetition of a sound by the reflection of sound waves

Exercise 2   Use one of the following words to complete each sentence about the story. Change word forms as needed.

bewildered   bounce   creep   inspect   kneel   muffle   starve

1.   Lennie claimed that he didn't _____ the puppy hard enough to kill it, but he must have handled it too roughly.

2.   Lennie _____ the puppy, looking closely at it.

3.   Curley's wife got down on her knees in the hay. She _____ next to Lennie to talk to him.

4. Lennie covered the girl's mouth to _____ the sound of her screams.

5. At first Lennie was _____ to see Curley's wife lying so still. Then he understood why she lay there like that.

6. Lennie crouched low as he _____ quietly to the wall of the barn and looked out through a crack at the men playing horseshoes.

7. George was convinced that if Lennie ran away on his own, he wouldn't be able to find anything to eat. He'd _____.

Exercise 3 Use the same words to complete these sentences, which are *not* related to the story. Change word forms as needed.

bewildered   bounce   creep   inspect   kneel   muffle   starve

1. The muffler on the car had a hole in it, so it didn't _____ the noise of the engine very well.

2. In some religions, people _____ when they pray.

3. When a basketball loses air, it doesn't _____ very high.

4. After engineers _____ the bridge, they declared that it was not safe to use.

5. The announcements coming over the loudspeaker system were impossible to understand. Everyone was _____, and they asked each other, "What was that? What did they say?"

6. The cat _____ through the tall grass towards the little bird.

7. The little girl in the car cried, "Please can we stop at McDonald's for something to eat? I'm _____!"

NOUNS	VERBS	ADJECTIVES	ADVERBS
_____	impress	_____ _____	

Exercise 4   Use your dictionary to complete the chart above. Then fill in each blank with the appropriate member of this word family.

1.   Curley's wife tried to _____ Lennie.

2.   Her story didn't make much of an _____ on him.

3.   Curley's wife thought he should be _____ by her connections to Hollywood.

4.   Lennie didn't think it was an _____ story. In fact, he probably didn't understand half of what she said.

Exercise 5   When would you . . .

1. ____ **console** someone?

2. ____ **confide in** someone?

3. ____ **impress** someone?

a.   when you trusted that person enough to say something personal

b.   when you showed some special talent, ability, or knowledge

c.   when that person had suffered a loss

> **rock**
>
> a. *(v.)* to (make something) move back and forth or side to
>   side repeatedly
>
> b. *(n.)* stone, a hard mineral substance
>
> c. *(n.)* rock 'n' roll music

Exercise 6   Look at the box above. Which meaning does "rock" have in each of the following sentences? Write the letter of the definition next to each sentence.

_____ **1.** Do you listen to **rock**?

_____ **2.** He **rocked** his baby to sleep in the old rocking chair.

_____ **3.** The ocean waves crashed against the **rocks**.

TEST YOURSELF

VOCABULARY REVIEW FOR CHAPTER 4, PARTS 1 AND 2

1. Are the underlined words in these pairs of sentences similar or different in meaning? Circle the letters of the pairs that are similar.

   a. They <u>get along</u> together.

   They <u>show up</u> together.

   b. It was an important <u>victory</u>.

   It was an important <u>win</u>.

   c. She <u>broke in</u> with a comment.

   She <u>interrupted</u> with a comment.

   d. He treated us <u>brutally</u>.

   He treated us <u>casually</u>.

   e. I <u>suppose</u> that it is true.

   I <u>imagine</u> that it is true.

   f. She was clearly <u>indignant</u>.

   She was clearly <u>miserable</u>.

2. Find and circle the words in this puzzle that are defined below. Words are written going down, across from left to right, or diagonally. Write each word you find next to its definition.

```
O  W  S  U  L  L  E  N  I
V  T  X  H  E  A  V  E  N
E  O  H  A  R  V  E  S  T
R  R  K  W  R  M  N  K  E
W  T  V  K  J  I  G  Z  N
H  U  H  B  P  M  G  X  S
E  R  W  L  E  A  N  H  I
L  E  J  Z  F  X  C  T  T
M  K  Z  G  U  I  L  T  Y
```

a. _ _ _ _ = thin, without any fat

b. _ _ _ _ _ = moral or legal claim

c. _ _ _ _ _ _ = being or feeling at fault or to blame for something

d. _ _ _ _ _ _ = silently showing resentment or a bad mood

e. _ _ _ _ _ _ = place of perfect happiness

f. _ _ _ _ _ _ _ _ = intentionally cause severe pain to

g. _ _ _ _ _ _ _ = gathering of crops

h. _ _ _ _ _ _ _ _ _ _ = strength, forcefulness, power

i. _ _ _ _ _ _ _ _ _ _ = overpower or overcome

3. Unscramble these words. (Their definitions follow in parentheses.)

    a. crons = _ _ _ _ _ (strong disrespect, contempt)

    b. mearf = _ _ _ _ _ (make someone seem guilty of a crime by lying, bringing false proofs, etc.)

    c. traubl = _ _ _ _ _ _ (cruel, without mercy)

    d. laebiirrt = _ _ _ _ _ _ _ _ _ (easily annoyed or made angry)

4. Circle three words from the following list that you could use to complete the sentence.

    aloof   bore   frame   lean   scornful   torture

Crooks was _____.

❧ Chapter Six ❧

(pages 99–107)

BEFORE YOU READ

ON YOUR OWN

Reading

Read this final chapter *without stopping*.

A Closer Look

1. Who are the two imaginary characters with whom Lennie talks while he waits for George?

2. What does Lennie expect George to say and do when he comes?

3. What does George do?

4. What do you think about what George does?

5. What future do you see for George?

Write any questions *you* have about this chapter.

DISCUSSION

1. Why does George lie about Lennie's having the gun?

2. Compare Slim and Carlson's reactions to what has happened.

3. Did George do the right thing? Explain your answers.

4. In the world that George knew, there was no good place for someone like Lennie. What about our world today: What happens to people like Lennie? How do *you* think we should we take care of people like Lennie?

5. About the title: Steinbeck took the title for this novel from a poem by Robert Burns, "To a Mouse On Turning Her Up in Her Nest with a Plow, November, 1785." In this poem, a farmer plowing a field accidentally digs up the underground nest of a mouse. She runs away in fright as the farmer apologizes for destroying the home she had built for the winter. Burns writes:

> The best-laid schemes o' mice an' men,
>> Gang aft a-gley,
> An' lea'e us naught but grief an' pain,
>> For promised joy!

Burns says that the most carefully made plans—people's plans as well as those of mice—often go wrong, leaving only sadness and pain in place of the happiness expected. Some people might conclude from this that it is useless, or even foolish, to make plans.

Read the following two statements and decide if either of them expresses your ideas about life. Tell what you believe and explain why you believe it.

- It is useless to plan and scheme because you cannot control the future and you will only be disappointed. Just take life as it comes.

- We can and we must shape our lives through the choices and plans we make. With hard work, we can all achieve our goals.

SUGGESTIONS FOR WRITING

Personal Response

Look back at your answer to the question on page 1: How do you feel about reading a novel in English?

In your journal, comment on what you wrote then and reflect on your experience reading this novel.

Summarizing

Activity 1 Write a summary of the novel. Limit your summary to no more than 200 words.

Activity 2　Chart the events in Chapters 4, 5, and 6 of the novel as you did on page 76 of the *Companion*:

Chapter	When	Where	What happens
4			
5			
6			

Points of Departure

1. Write a letter to a new student in which you describe the novel. (Be sure that you don't give away the ending!) Tell your reader whether or not you recommend the novel and why.

2. How much can we plan our lives? How much should we try to? Explain your opinion, giving examples (from the novel or from your own experiences) to support what you say.

3. Describe the relationship between George and Lennie. Be sure to give examples from the novel to support your statements about them. What would Lennie's life have been like without George? What is George's life going to be like without Lennie?

4. How are the killing of Candy's dog and the killing of Lennie similar? How are they different?

5. Choose a character from the novel who interests you. What is your opinion of this person? Support your statements with examples from the novel of things this character does or says. How is this person important to the story?

6. Write a different ending for the novel. Choose the point in the story where you want to begin, and tell the story from that point as you imagine it happening differently.

WORDS TO KNOW

shiver *(v.)* Afterwards, George **shivered**.

107   **a whisper** *(n.)* When George answered Carlson's question, his voice was almost a **whisper**.

Exercise 1   Use one of the following words to complete each sentence about the story. Change word forms as needed.

gigantic   moan   monotonous   retort   shiver   whisper

1.   Lennie felt such grief that he _____, expressing his pain and sadness in a long, low, wordless sound.

2.   Out of Lennie's imagination came a _____ rabbit which sat up in front of him and scolded him.

3.   The rabbit said George would beat Lennie with a stick, but Lennie _____, "George won't do nothing like that."

4.   George's voice was _____: he couldn't put any feeling or emphasis into the words he was repeating.

5.   After the shooting, George _____, reacting involuntarily to what he had done.

6.   George managed to give answers to Carlson's questions but his voice was so low that it was almost a _____.

Exercise 2   Use the same words in these sentences, which are *not* related to the story. Change word forms as needed.

gigantic   moan   monotonous   retort   shiver   whisper

1.   You must be cold—I can see that you are _____.

2.   The planet Jupiter is so _____ that all the other planets of our solar system together do not equal it in size.

3. I couldn't hear what the doctor told my parents about me because she spoke to them in a _____.

4. Some factory workers have jobs that require doing the same thing over and over again. These jobs must be _____.

5. I woke up when I heard my sister _____ in her sleep. She was having a bad dream.

6. When my brother criticized me for keeping everyone waiting, I _____ that we had all waited for *him* plenty of times!

Exercise 3 Choose the best adverb to describe how each person would act or behave.

dutifully   frantically   shakily

1. a mother in a panic, looking for her lost child _____

2. a person who was weak from a long illness _____

3. a son following his father's instructions _____

NOUNS	VERBS	ADJECTIVES	ADVERBS
triumph	_____	_____	_____

Exercise 4 Use your dictionary to complete the chart above. Then fill in each blank with the appropriate member of this word family.

1. In spite of all his troubles, Lennie cried out in _____ because he still had George.

2. Lennie finished George's sentence in a _____ voice.

3. George seemed to feel there was no way they could ever _____ over their difficulties.

NOUNS	VERBS	ADJECTIVES	ADVERBS
_____	steady	_____	_____

Exercise 5   Use your dictionary to complete the chart above. Then fill in each blank with the appropriate member of this word family.

1.   The ladder wasn't _____, so I didn't want to climb it.

2.   We worked _____ until the job was done.

3.   Everyone admires him for the _____ of his nerves when he is under pressure.

4.   ". . . George raised the gun and _____ it, . . ." (106).

TEST YOURSELF

VOCABULARY REVIEW FOR CHAPTERS 5 & 6

1. Which word does not belong in the group? Cross it out.

    a. moan   chuckle   creep   whisper

    b. shiver   tremble   shake   steady

    c. discontented   dutiful   dissatisfied   miserable

    d. retort   triumph   victory   success

2. Are the underlined words in these pairs of sentences similar or different in meaning? Circle the letters of the pairs that are similar.

    a. What he saw bewildered him.

       What he saw confused him.

    b. She cried out frantically.

       She cried out in a panic.

    c. He made a retort.

       He made a threat.

    d. The patient moaned.

       The patient grinned.

    e. He is a dutiful son.

       He is a responsible son.

3. Use the clues given below to fill in the words in the puzzle.

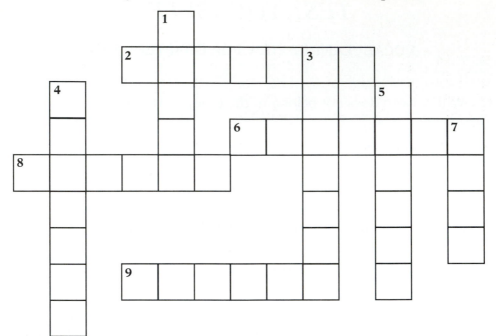

ACROSS

2. look at carefully, examine
6. give comfort or sympathy to (someone who is sad)
8. make less loud by covering with something
9. die of hunger

DOWN

1. get down on or be on one's knees
3. tell (something personal or secret) to a trusted person
4. laugh quietly
5. make something, such as a ball, hit and spring back up (from the ground, the floor, etc.)
7. a sound repeated because of sound waves being reflected off a surface and sent back

All the words used in the puzzle can be found in this list.

bounce	echo	rock
chuckle	frantic	shiver
confide	impress	sorrow
console	inspect	starve
creep	kneel	triumph
dutiful	muffle	whisper

4. Answer these questions about the story.

   a. Who was eager to **impress** people? _____

   b. Who **rocked** back and forth in **sorrow**? _____

   c. What was **gigantic**? _____

   d. Who cried out in **triumph**? _____

   e. Who spoke in a **monotonous** voice? _____

   f. What did George need to **steady**? _____

Answer Key

CHAPTER 1: PART 1

PAGE   **Exercises**
11–13   **1.**   1) a path 2) a paw 3) brush
           2.   1) emerged 2) denim 3) imitate 4) morosely
                    5) scowled 6) grinned
           3.   1) imitate 2) grinning 3) morosely 4) scowls 5) denim
                    6) emerge
           4.   1) a, 2) c, 3) b
           5.   1) *n.,* 2) *v.,* 3) *v.,* 4) *n.,* 5) *n.,* 6) *v.*

CHAPTER 1: PART 2

21   **Summarizing**
           1) B, 2) C, 3) C, 4) B, 5) B and C

           Exercises
23–26   **1.**   1) remind 2) sneaked 3) cave 4) look after 5) by
                    heart 6) tend
           2.   1) tends 2) look after 3) cave 4) by heart 5) remind
                    6) sneak
           3.   1) disgusted 2) disgustedly 3) reluctantly
                    4) reluctant 5) ashamed 6) ashamedly
           4.   1) b, 2) c, 3) a
           5.   1) c, 2) a, 3) b, 4) d

CHAPTER 2: PART 1

41–44   **Exercises**
           1.   1) show off 2) scoff at 3) shuffle 4) squirm
           2.   1) panic 2) stake 3) get away with 4) struggle
                    5) reassured 6) gossip

3. 1) reassured 2) panic 3) gossip 4) stake 5) get away with
   6) struggled

4. 1) different 2) similar 3) different 4) different 5) similar

5. 1) skeptical 2) skeptically 3) skepticism 4) skeptic

6. *n.:* calculation, calculator; *v.:* calculate 1) calculating
   2) calculated 3) calculator 4) calculations

7. 1, 2, 3, 6, and 8 are verbs; 4, 5, and 7 are nouns

CHAPTER 2: PART 2

53–55   **Exercises**

1. 1) authority 2) dignity 3) a compliment

2. 1) brusquely 2) fascinated 3) apprehensive 4) drowned
   5) precede 6) insultingly

3. 1) apprehensive 2) insultingly 3) brusquely 4) preceded
   5) fascinated 6) drowned

4. *n.:* fascination, *v.:* fascinate 1) fascinating 2) fascinated

5. *n.:* insult, *v.:* insult, *adj.:* insulted, insulting 1) insulting
   2) insulted

6. 1) c, 2) a, 3) b

56–58   **TEST YOURSELF — CHAPTER 1**

1. a, d, and g are similar

2. ACROSS: 3. mean, 6. disgust, 7. path

   DOWN: 1. remind, 2. paw, 4. brush, 5. pet

3. a) George and Lennie's coats and trousers b) George
   c) a dead mouse d) leaving Weed e) Lennie f) the story
   of the house and land they're going to have someday

CHAPTER 3: PART 1

68–70   **Exercises**

1. 1) a crop 2) lynch 3) a barn 4) rape

2. 1) keep up with 2) defensively 3) nuisance 4) conceal
   5) uneasily 6) get it over with

3. 1) conceals 2) keep up with 3) get it over with
   4) defensively 5) nuisance 6) uneasily

4. 1) d, 2) a, 3) b, 4) c

5. *n.:* apology, *adj.:* apologetic, *adv.:* apologetically
   1) apologized 2) apologetically 3) apologetic 4) apology

6. 1) b, 2) c, 3) a

CHAPTER 3: PART 2

79–81   **Exercises**

1. 1) bruise 2) an acre 3) retreat 4) sigh

2. 1) shows up 2) subsided 3) rage 4) fist 5) crouched
   6) fault

3. 1) crouched 2) show up 3) subsided 4) rage 5) fault
   6) fist

4. 1) different 2) different 3) similar 4) different

5. *n.:* threat, *v.:* threaten, *adj.:* threatening 1) threateningly
   2) threatening 3) threat 4) threatened

6. 1) b, 2) a, 3) c

82–84   **TEST YOURSELF—CHAPTER 2**

1. b) reassured him. c) stared at him. d) fascinated him.
   e) complimented him. f) preceded him out of the bunk
   house.

2. a) drown b) crooked c) shuffle d) struggle e) authority

3. a) the boss, b) Curley, c) Candy, Whit, d) Curley,
   e) George, f) Curley's wife, Lennie

4. b) stink c) stake d) bright e) dignity f) insulting
   g) skeptical h) derogatory i) confidence

CHAPTER 4: PART 1

90–93   **Exercises**

1. 1) a victory 2) torture 3) heaven

2. 1) aloof 2) lean 3) bore 4) suppose 5) approached
   6) scornful

3. 1) bore 2) Suppose 3) lean 4) scornful 5) approached
   6) aloof

4. *v.:* intensify, *adj.:* intense, *adv.:* intensely 1) intense
   2) intensity 3) intensified 4) intensely

5. 1) d, 2) b, 3) a, 4) c

6. 1) b, 2) c, 3) a

CHAPTER 4: PART 2

102–105 **Exercises**

1. 1) harvest 2) overwhelmed 3) got along 4) sullen
   5) indignation

2. 1) gotten along 2) overwhelmed 3) indignation 4) sullen
   5) harvest

3. 1) irritably 2) brutally 3) guiltily

4. 1) brutal 2) guilty 3) irritable

5. 1) irritable 2) irritated 3) irritating

6. 1) b, 2) a, 3) c

7. 1) c, 2) a, 3) b

106–108 **TEST YOURSELF—CHAPTER 3**

1. a) show up. b) keep up with him. c) stand it. d) get it
   over with. e) retreat.

2. b, c, and f are similar

3. a) F, b) T, c) F, d) F, e) T, f) F, g) T

4. ACROSS: 2. subside, 4. nuisance, 6. fist, 7. fault, 8. sigh

   DOWN: 1. rage, 3. bruise, 5. crouch

CHAPTER 5

116–119 **Exercises**

1. 1) sorrow 2) chuckle 3) discontent 4) echo

2. 1) bounce 2) inspected 3) knelt 4) muffle 5) bewildered
   6) crept 7) starve

3. 1) muffle 2) kneel 3) bounce 4) inspected 5) bewildered
   6) crept 7) starved/starving

4. *n.:* impression, *adj.:* impressed, impressive 1) impress 2) impression 3) impressed 4) impressive

5. 1) c, 2) a, 3) b

6. 1) c, 2) a, 3) b

120–122 **TEST YOURSELF—CHAPTER 4**

1. b, c, and e are similar

2. a) lean b) right c) guilty d) sullen e) heaven f) torture g) harvest h) intensity i) overwhelm

3. a) scorn b) frame c) brutal d) irritable

4. aloof, lean, scornful

CHAPTER 6

130–132 **Exercises**

1. 1) moaned 2) gigantic 3) retorted 4) monotonous 5) shivered 6) whisper

2. 1) shivering 2) gigantic 3) whisper 4) monotonous 5) moan 6) retorted

3. 1) frantically 2) shakily 3) dutifully

4. *v.:* triumph, *adj.:* triumphant, *adv.:* triumphantly 1) triumph 2) triumphant 3) triumph

5. *n.:* steadiness, *adj.:* steady, *adv.:* steadily 1) steady 2) steadily 3) steadiness 4) steadied

133–135 **TEST YOURSELF—CHAPTERS 5 AND 6**

1. a) creep b) steady c) dutiful d) retort

2. a, b, and e are similar

3. ACROSS: 2. inspect, 6. console, 8. muffle, 9. starve

   DOWN: 1. kneel, 3. confide, 4. chuckle, 5. bounce, 7. echo

4. a) Curley's wife b) Lennie c) the rabbit d) Lennie e) George f) his hand/the gun

TEACHING SUGGESTIONS

There are many ways that you, the instructor, might use this *Companion*. It is meant to be a versatile tool in your hands. Following are a few suggestions.

Starting Out

The questions in this section can help make you and the students aware of the ideas that each reader brings to the novel. Students can discuss the questions in small groups, or you can make this a Think/Pair/Share activity by giving the class a minute to think or write about a question, then having pairs of students share their ideas with their partners. Each pair then joins another pair, a larger group, or the whole class for follow-up. This technique enriches discussion and allows all the members of a class to take part.

Before You Read

Have the students read this section silently in class before beginning each reading assignment in the novel. They can then ask questions before going on with the reading outside of class.

Reading Aloud

Reading aloud to the class at the beginning of the novel or a new section of it is an effective and pleasurable way to get students started. Your reading aloud is also useful when a particular passage confuses students, as the stress and intonation you give to the passage may clarify its meaning for them without your having to resort to explaining or interpreting.

The Novel on Tape

An audiotape recording of the novel read by Gary Sinese is available from the HighBridge Company by calling (800) 755–8532 or by writing to the company at 100 Westgate Dr., St. Paul, MN 55114. This recording consists of two tapes with a running time of three hours. The novel has been abridged by omitting the last part of the second chapter and the first part of the third. There is also a 60-minute dramatization of the novel available on audiotape from National Recording Company, P.O. Box 395, Glenview, IL 60025.

The Novel on Film

An excellent film version of the novel was made in 1992 and is available on video. It stars John Malkovich as Lennie and Gary Sinese as George. Consider showing it after finishing the novel.

On Your Own

Have the students write their answers to the questions in A Closer Look. Writing will consolidate their understanding of the material and help them sort out their thoughts about it. Depending on their level, you can urge, even require, that students use their own words rather than quotations.

Students can write their answers on separate sheets of paper to be handed in; or they can write them in the *Companion* for you to collect periodically. If the students hand in written responses, you can scan their work quickly (while students begin working in groups) to look for misconceptions about the novel or for questions students have written to you.

In class, review some of the questions from A Closer Look to lay a foundation for group discussions.

Scenes from the Novel

On pages 36 and 62 are excerpts from Steinbeck's *Of Mice and Men: A Play in Three Acts*. These can be read aloud by students in small groups or by volunteers in front of the class. On page 99, students are directed to mark their books to create a script themselves. (At this point, the play differs markedly from the novel.) If students enjoy the readings, they can adapt conversations from other parts of the novel for more role-plays.

Discussion

You may wish to keep the entire class together for most discussion, especially if there are fewer than ten students. Try the Think/Pair/Share technique described under Starting Out.

In larger classes, small-group work promotes involvement in the discussion and helps foster in students an increased responsibility for their own learning. Groups of four or five students are small enough for students to manage and large enough to promise a variety of perspectives, particularly if you can set up groups that are mixed in terms of academic proficiency, English skills, first language, and cultural background.

The need to produce something concrete, such as written answers to questions, and the prospect of reporting back to the class will give each group a clear purpose.

For balanced participation by all group members, have each student in a group be responsible for a particular role, with students changing roles at each meeting. Here are some suggested roles and their responsibilities:

- The Facilitator opens discussion, makes sure that each group member has a chance to speak, and sees that no one person dominates.

- The Recorder writes down the group's response(s) to each question.

- The Checker makes sure that members of the group understand each other and helps the Recorder as needed.

- The Timekeeper helps the group stay focused by keeping track of the time allotted for the discussion and the time they are spending on each question.

- The Spokesperson reports on the group's discussion when the entire class reconvenes, referring as needed to what the Recorder has written.

You can give each group a folder containing a handout describing these responsibilities and a sign-up sheet to help students keep track of the roles they assume.

Students must understand these roles well if they are to take them seriously and succeed in breaking out of patterns of group work in which a few students dominate. You can help by insisting that only the Recorder write on the group answer sheet and that only the Spokesperson speak for the group (until you open up the discussion to everyone in the class), and by eliciting feedback from the students on their experiences in these roles.

For more information on Cooperative Learning, see *Learning Together and Alone* by David W. Johnson and Roger T. Johnson (1991, Allyn & Bacon) and *Cooperative Learning: Increasing College Faculty Instructional Productivity* by David W. Johnson, Roger T. Johnson, and Karl A. Smith (1991, The George Washington University).

Role-Plays   The following ideas for role-plays do not require writing scripts or memorizing lines. After the students have read at least through Chapter 3 of the novel and are familiar with the characters, you can do any of these.

Panel: Have pairs of students assume the roles of characters. (Two students sharing one role may feel less pressured and generate more ideas and more talk.) Give the students a few minutes to discuss their character with their partner. Then have all the students sit in a circle or semicircle with the partners together. Each pair in turn introduces themselves, and the other students ask questions for them to answer in character.

Small-Group Interview: Have several volunteers assume the roles of characters from the story. Let them leave the room (with their books) to talk over what they know and imagine about their characters. Lead the rest of the class in brainstorming questions to ask these characters, and write these sample questions on the board. Divide the class into small groups, preferably of three or four students each, making as many groups as there are characters. Invite the role-players back into the room, asking each of them to join a group. Each group can then interview their character. Have the role-players change groups every few minutes.

Mingling: Give each student a slip of paper with a character's name on it. The student assumes the identity of that character. Everyone circulates freely around the room asking Yes/No questions until they have enough information to guess the identities of the other students. Each student is allowed only one guess at the identity of each of the other characters.

Points of Departure

How you assign these topics will depend on your objective. If your goal is to develop students' fluency in written English and help them understand the reading, then use these topics for informal assignments, such as journal entries or freewriting in class. In these cases, you would address grammar and other aspects of accuracy in written English only when the writer's meaning was obscured. (Note: Some of these topics are good for freewriting *before* students read the chapter.)

For more formal compositions, you will need to guide students through the stages of the writing process: from discussion of the assignment through prewriting, composing, sharing their drafts with you or their peers, revising, and editing. In order to maintain momentum in reading the novel, have the students carry such an assignment only partway through the process and then put aside their drafts until after they finish the novel. Then they can complete the revising and editing stages.

Words to Know

These exercises lend themselves to independent work by students. Once students have studied the vocabulary, review it in class. At the least demanding level: Ask students to open their *Companions* to a list of WORDS TO KNOW and say, "Quickly, find a word that means . . .," or "Tell me a word that describes how Lennie . . . ." For a more demanding review, post a list of the words on the wall or blackboard and ask students to speak about the meaning of each word and its use in the story.

The emphasis in the vocabulary exercises is on developing students' *understanding* of words they read. The students will need additional practice and guidance to be able to *use* the words in speaking and writing.

Assessment

Possibilities include:

Requiring portfolios based on the novel: Portfolios can include homework assignments, journal entries, in-class writing, essays, samples of group work, and the student's reflections on the process of reading the novel with the class.

Giving quizzes on the novel: Quizzes can include vocabulary exercises (which may be taken directly from the *Companion*); questions about the plot; exercises on matching quotations and the characters who spoke the lines or who are described in them; and lists of important people, places, and things from the novel which students must identify.

Having students create quizzes: Groups of students can make up questions about the novel to hand in to you. Choose questions from each group to create a test.

Giving an open-book exam: Give students a choice of essay topics (which may be drawn from the Discussion or Points of Departure sections of the *Companion*). They should find support in the novel for statements they make and include page references in their essays.

WORDS TO KNOW

Companion page numbers are given in parentheses.

A
acre (77)
aloof (89)
apologize (67)
apprehensive (52)
approach (90)
ashamedly (22)
authority (52)

B
barn (66)
bewildered (115)
bore (89)
bounce (114)
break in (101)
bright (40)
bruise (78)
brush (10)
brusquely (51)
brutally (101)
by heart (23)

C
calculating (40)
can't stand (67)
casually (77)
cave (23)
chuckle (115)
compliment (52)
conceal (67)
confide (115)
confidence (52)
console (115)
creep (115)
crooked (39)
crop (66)
crouch (78)

D
defensively (66)
denim (11)
derogatory (41)
dignity (52)
discontent (116)
disgustedly (22)
drown (52)
dutifully (129)

E
eagerly (78)
echo (116)
emerge (10)
entranced (78)

F
fascinated (51)
fault (78)
fist (78)
frame (101)
frantically (129)

G
get along (with) (101)
get away with (40)
get (something) over
    with (67)
gigantic (129)
gossip (40)
grin (11)
guiltily (101)

H
harm (67)
harvest (101)
heaven (90)

I
imitate (11)
impress (115)
indignation (101)
inspect (114)
insultingly (52)
intensity (89)
irritably (101)

K
keep up with (66)
kind (67)
kneel (115)

L
lean (89)
look after (23)
lynch (67)

M
mean (23)
miserably (78)
moan (129)
monotonous (129)
morosely (11)
muffle (115)

N
nuisance (66)

O
overwhelm (101)

P
panic (39)
path (10)
paw (11)

pet   (11)
precede   (52)

R
rage   (78)
rape   (66)
reassure   (40)
reluctantly   (22)
remind   (22)
retort   (129)
retreat   (78)
right   (89)
rock   (115)

S
scoff at   (39)
scornful   (90)
scowl   (11)
shakily   (129)
shiver   (130)
show off   (40)
show up   (77)
shuffle   (39)
sigh   (77)
skeptically   (39)
sneak   (22)
sorrow   (115)
squirm   (40)

stake   (40)
stare   (40)
starve   (116)
steady   (129)
stiff   (67)
still   (68)
stink   (52)
stroke   (22)
struggle   (40)
subside   (77)
sullenly   (101)
suppose   (89)

T
tend   (23)
threateningly   (77)
torture   (89)
triumph   (129)

U
uneasily   (67)

V
victory   (89)

W
whisper   (130)
will   (78)